Junior Mathematical Dom

36 activities for 7-1...

Tracey MacDonald

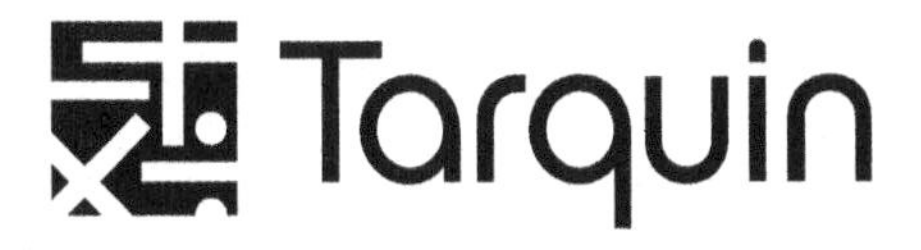
Tarquin

Dedication:

For Cara and Owen
With Love from Mummy x

www.tarquingroup.com
© 2017 Tracey Macdonald
ISBN: 978-1-907550-06-5

Distributed in the USA by Parkwest
www.parkwestpubs.com
www.amazon.com & major retailers

Printed and designed in the UK
Published by Tarquin Publications
Suite 74, 17 Holywell Hill
St Albans
AL1 1DT

Introduction and Instructions

Each set of dominoes is in the form of a master that can be photocopied and also provides a chain of answers. Sets need to be prepared in advance as students soon realise that keeping the cards in order as they cut them out means they can avoid attempting all the questions! Students could glue them down on completion so that they can be used as wall displays or 'spot the mistake' activities.

On each domino there is a half that shows an answer and another half with a question. The task is to correctly match up each question and answer in order to get the dominoes to form a continuous loop. Some sets loop clockwise but others go anti-clockwise.

Students can self or peer assess their work to some extent; thus reducing workload for the teacher. With increasing demand to make mathematics more interesting it also provides a fun activity that requires little writing for the students. The students can even be involved in making their own sets which they get to use again, share with other classes or display on the wall. Sets can be scanned into Interactive whiteboard packages so the students can manipulate them on the board as a collective activity or spot deliberate mistakes which you have engineered.

Alternatively, make an extra large set of dominoes and give the students one each. Ask them to create a 'human loop' using their cards. It gets them active and talking about mathematics. For some classes this might mean giving out two different sets and their first task would be to find the people with the other dominoes to make a set with theirs.

Blank domino templates for 12 and 18 domino activities are provided at the end of the book.

Tracey Macdonald

Addition Dominoes: 2 digit to 2 digit

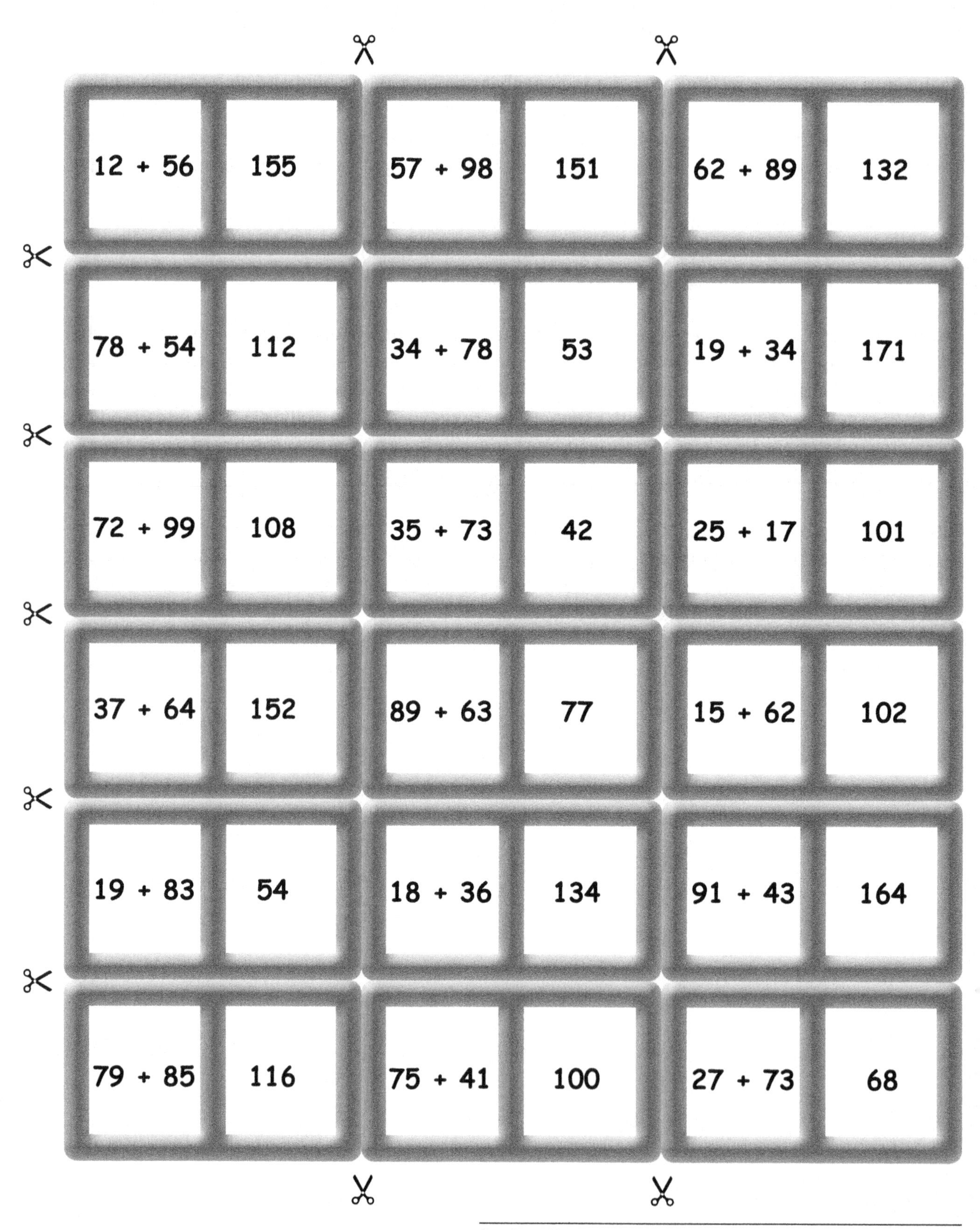

12 + 56	155	57 + 98	151	62 + 89	132
78 + 54	112	34 + 78	53	19 + 34	171
72 + 99	108	35 + 73	42	25 + 17	101
37 + 64	152	89 + 63	77	15 + 62	102
19 + 83	54	18 + 36	134	91 + 43	164
79 + 85	116	75 + 41	100	27 + 73	68

Addition Dominoes: 3 digit and 2 digit

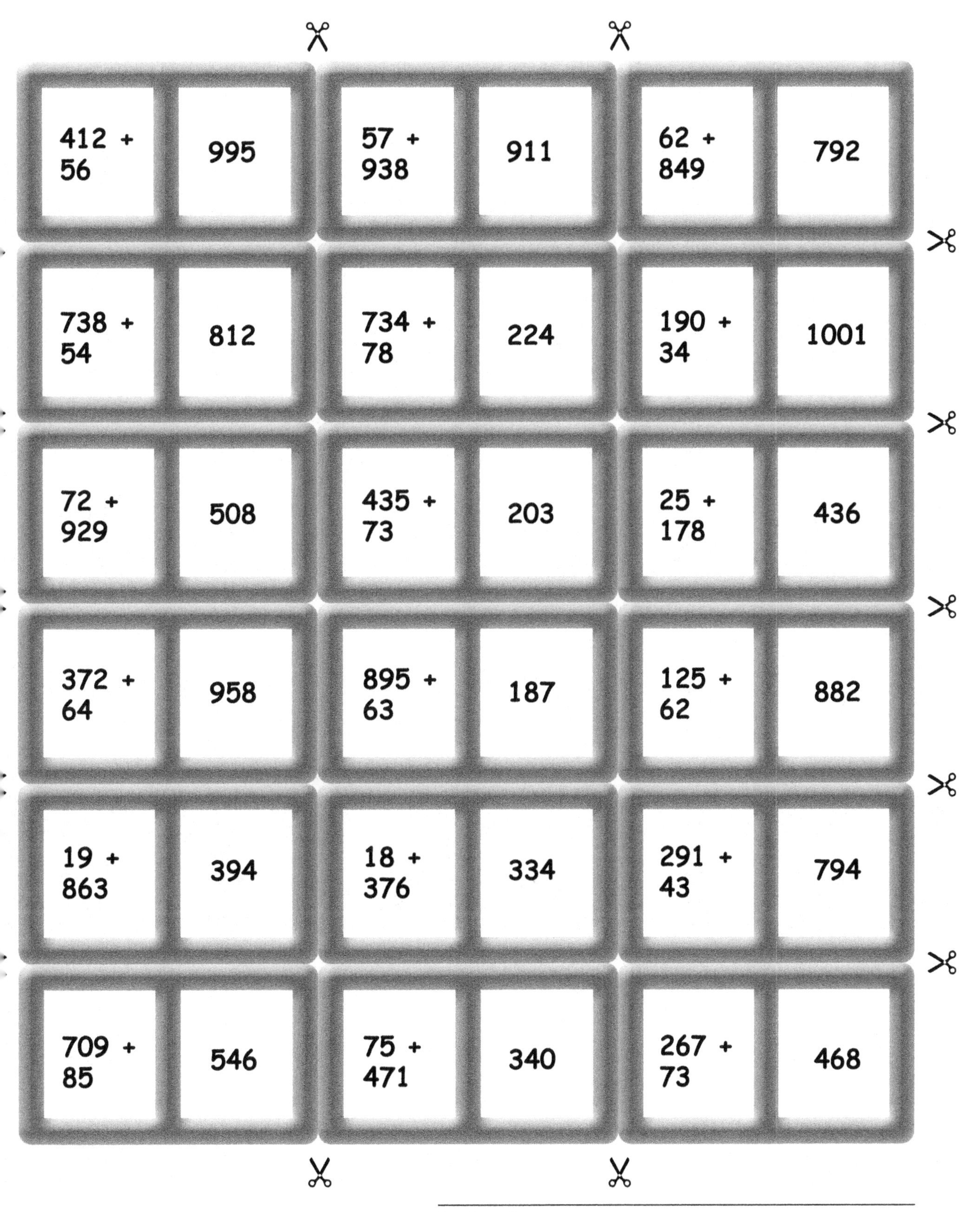

412 + 56	995	57 + 938	911	62 + 849	792
738 + 54	812	734 + 78	224	190 + 34	1001
72 + 929	508	435 + 73	203	25 + 178	436
372 + 64	958	895 + 63	187	125 + 62	882
19 + 863	394	18 + 376	334	291 + 43	794
709 + 85	546	75 + 471	340	267 + 73	468

Addition: 3 digit and 3 digit

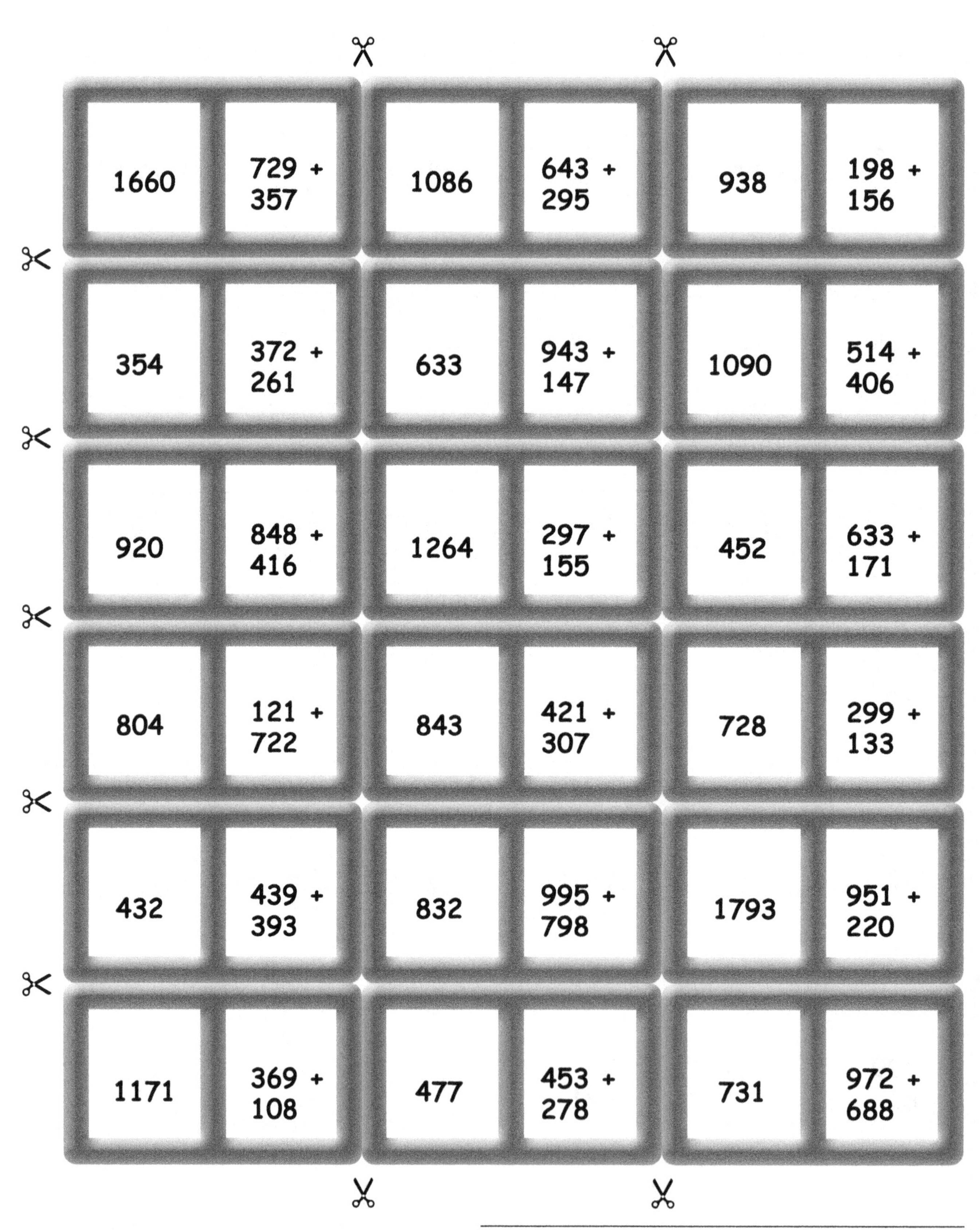

1660	729 + 357	1086	643 + 295	938	198 + 156
354	372 + 261	633	943 + 147	1090	514 + 406
920	848 + 416	1264	297 + 155	452	633 + 171
804	121 + 722	843	421 + 307	728	299 + 133
432	439 + 393	832	995 + 798	1793	951 + 220
1171	369 + 108	477	453 + 278	731	972 + 688

Area of Rectangles and Squares

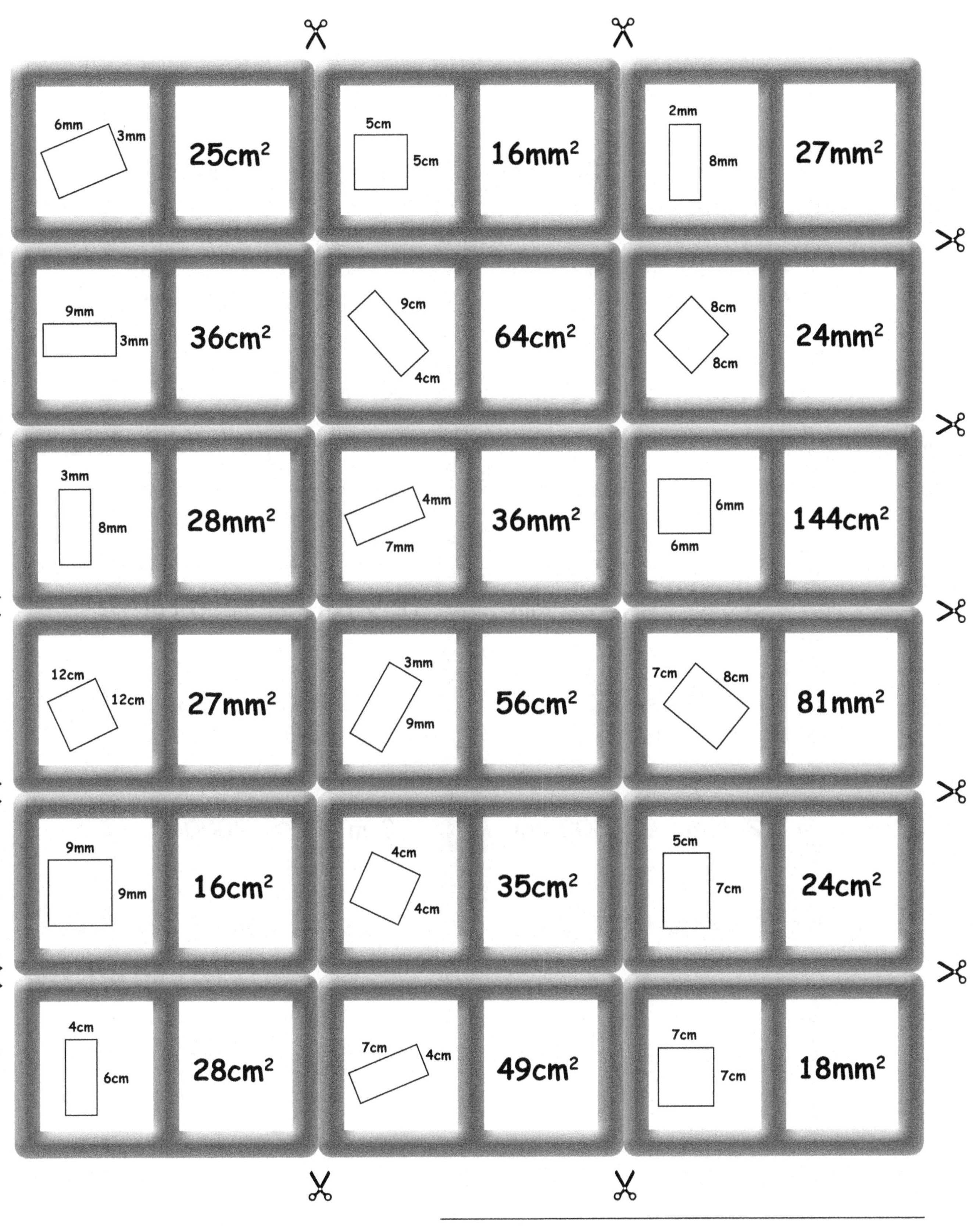

Metric Length Conversion Dominoes

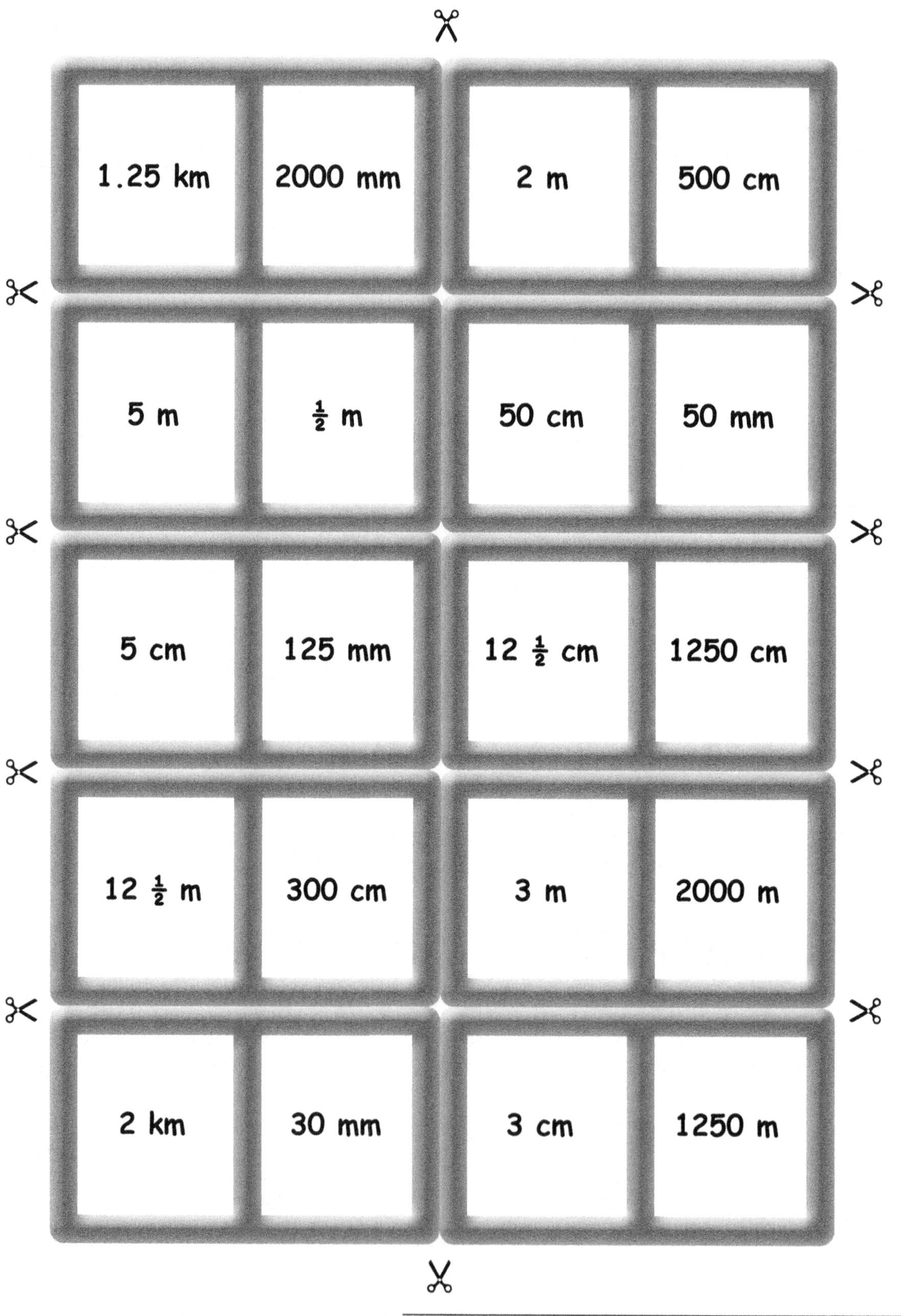

1.25 km	2000 mm	2 m	500 cm
5 m	½ m	50 cm	50 mm
5 cm	125 mm	12 ½ cm	1250 cm
12 ½ m	300 cm	3 m	2000 m
2 km	30 mm	3 cm	1250 m

Metric Volume

50 cl	10 ml	1 cl	1000 ml	1 litre (ℓ)	1750 ml
$1\frac{3}{4}$ litre (ℓ)	100 cl	1 litre (ℓ)	1500 ml	$1\frac{1}{2}$ litre (ℓ)	100 ml
10 cl	500 cl	5 litre (ℓ)	400 ml	40 cl	800 ml
0.8 litre (ℓ)	800 ml	80 cl	75 cl	$\frac{3}{4}$ litre (ℓ)	4000 ml
4 litre (ℓ)	50 cl	$\frac{1}{2}$ litre (ℓ)	1000 ml	100 cl	300 cl
3 litre (ℓ)	250 ml	$\frac{1}{4}$ litre (ℓ)	700 cl	7 litre (ℓ)	500 ml

Metric Weight

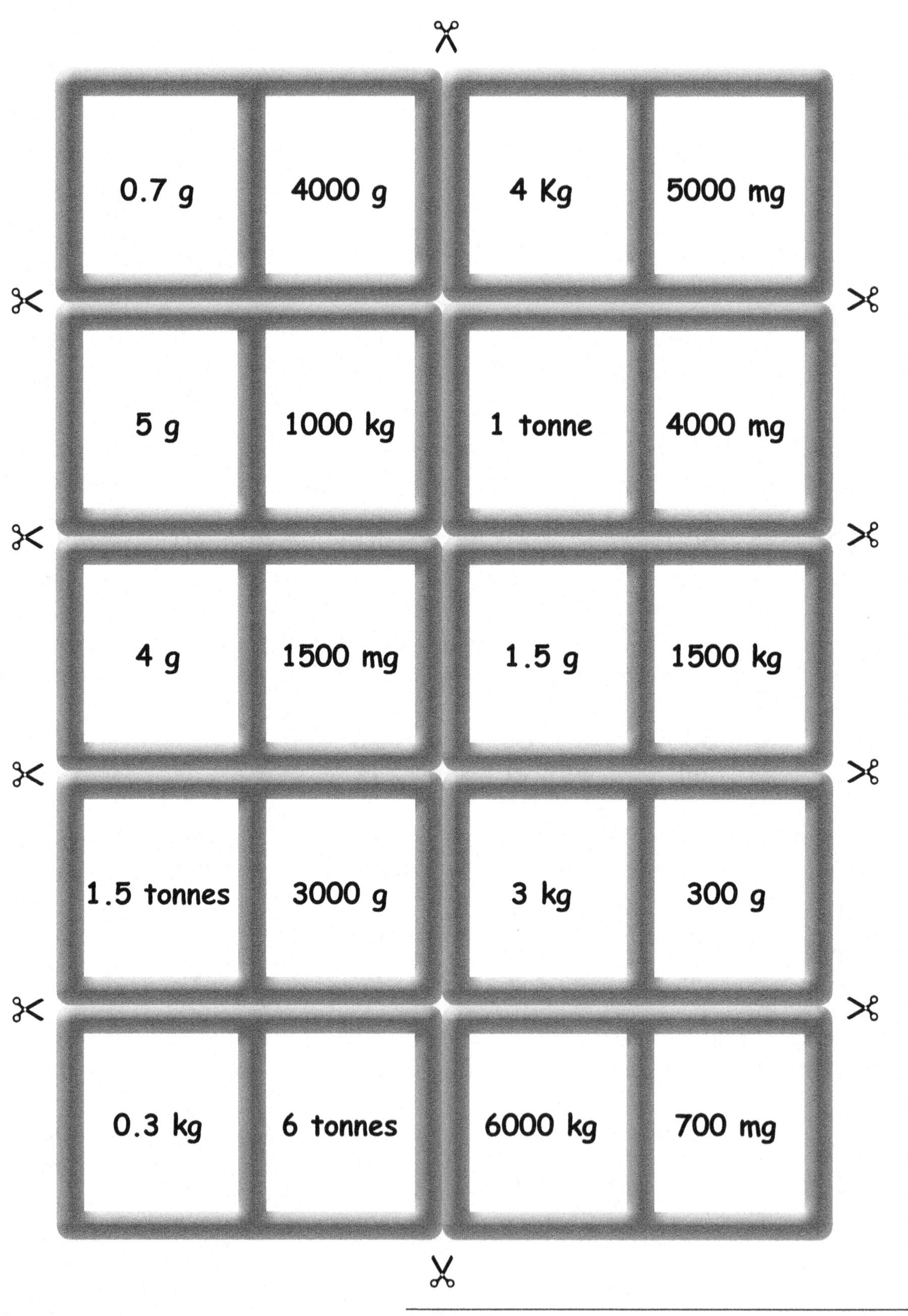

0.7 g	4000 g	4 Kg	5000 mg
5 g	1000 kg	1 tonne	4000 mg
4 g	1500 mg	1.5 g	1500 kg
1.5 tonnes	3000 g	3 kg	300 g
0.3 kg	6 tonnes	6000 kg	700 mg

Decimal Addition and Subtraction Dominoes

4.5	0.9 + 9.5	10.4	1.3 + 4.2	5.5	7.8 - 3.5
4.3	2.7 + 6.3	9.0	6.8 - 4.9	1.9	9.2 - 3.6
5.6	4.2 + 8.7	12.9	3.2 - 2.5	0.7	3.6 + 7.1
10.7	6.3 - 1.8	4.5	4.7 + 8.6	13.3	9.0 - 5.9
3.1	6.1 - 3.7	2.4	5.9 + 9.8	15.7	2.8 - 0.5
2.3	0.6 + 6.7	7.3	5.8 - 4.9	0.9	1.7 + 2.8

Student Sheet

Decimals Divided by 1 digit

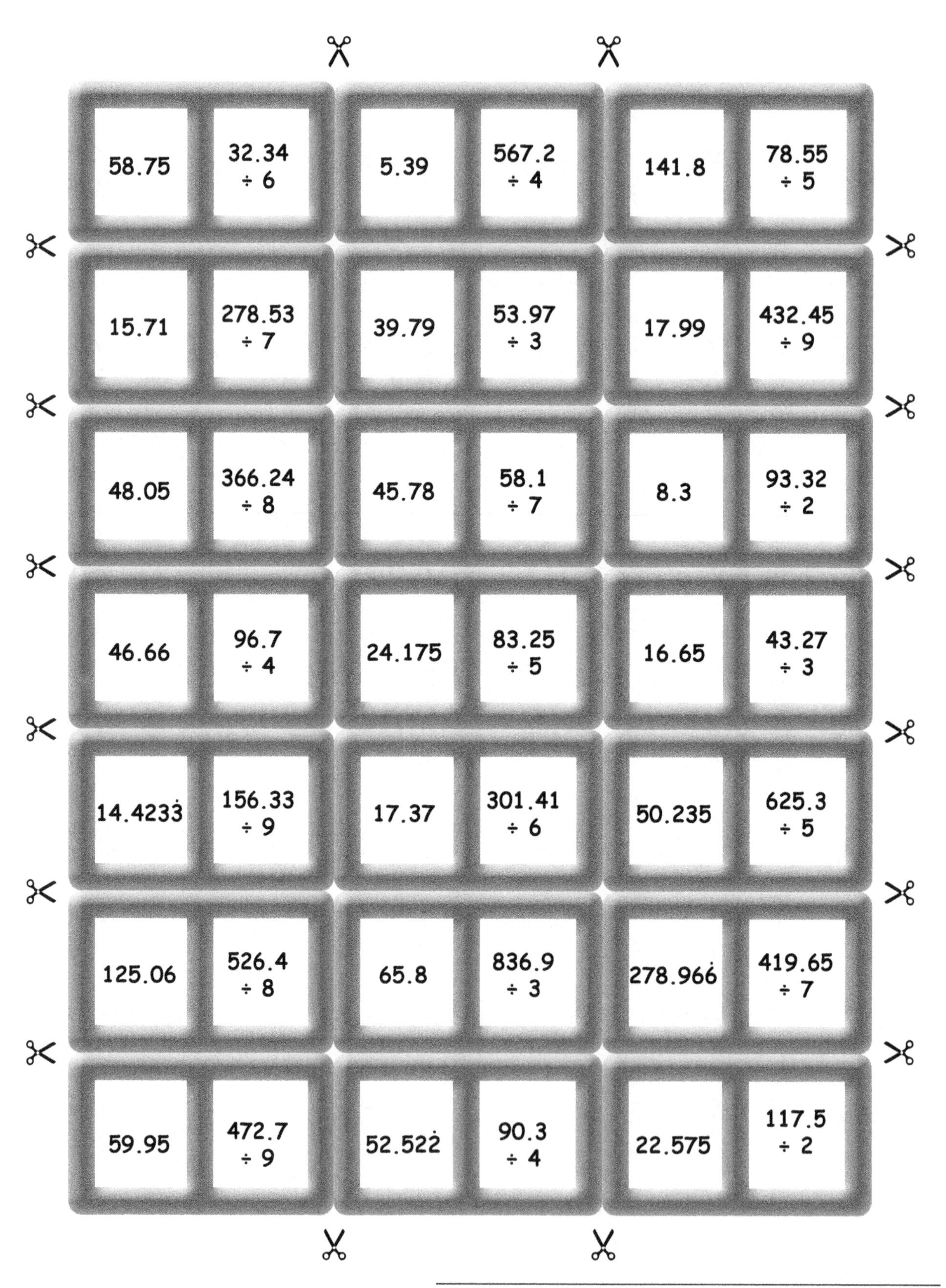

58.75	32.34 ÷ 6	5.39	567.2 ÷ 4	141.8	78.55 ÷ 5
15.71	278.53 ÷ 7	39.79	53.97 ÷ 3	17.99	432.45 ÷ 9
48.05	366.24 ÷ 8	45.78	58.1 ÷ 7	8.3	93.32 ÷ 2
46.66	96.7 ÷ 4	24.175	83.25 ÷ 5	16.65	43.27 ÷ 3
14.4233̇	156.33 ÷ 9	17.37	301.41 ÷ 6	50.235	625.3 ÷ 5
125.06	526.4 ÷ 8	65.8	836.9 ÷ 3	278.966̇	419.65 ÷ 7
59.95	472.7 ÷ 9	52.522̇	90.3 ÷ 4	22.575	117.5 ÷ 2

Student Sheet

Decimals: Divide by Powers of 10

0.033	37 ÷ 10	3.7	292 ÷ 100	2.92	4.5 ÷ 10
0.45	16 ÷ 1000	0.016	8 ÷ 100	0.08	1.6 ÷ 10
0.16	45 ÷ 1000	0.045	678 ÷ 10	67.8	29.2 ÷ 100
0.292	37 ÷ 1000	0.037	7 ÷ 100	0.07	8.9 ÷ 10
0.89	4612 ÷ 100	46.12	70 ÷ 1000	0.07	800 ÷ 1000
0.8	0.25 ÷ 10	0.025	461.2 ÷ 100	4.612	33 ÷ 1000

Decimals Multiplied by Powers of 10

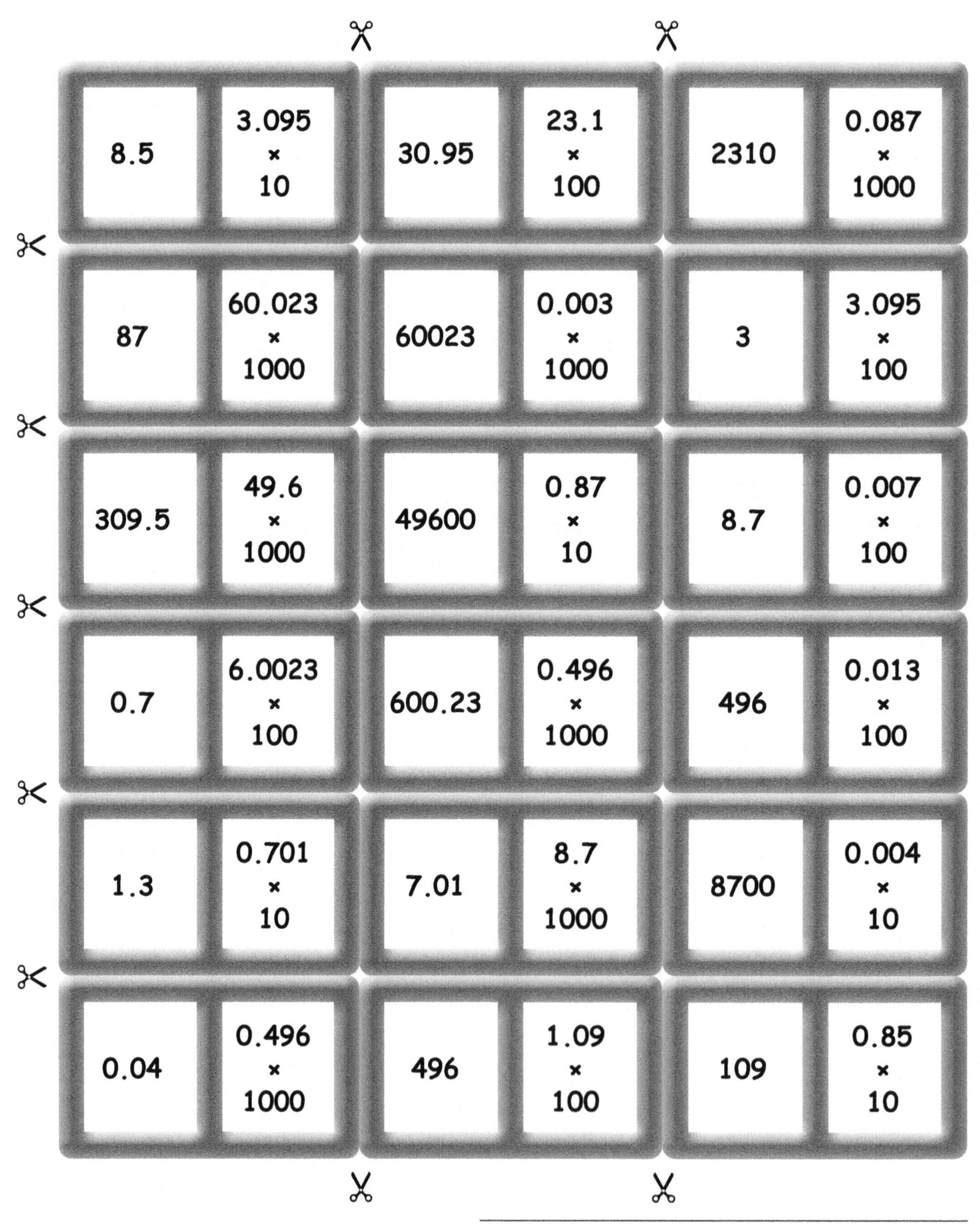

8.5	3.095 × 10	30.95	23.1 × 100	2310	0.087 × 1000
87	60.023 × 1000	60023	0.003 × 1000	3	3.095 × 100
309.5	49.6 × 1000	49600	0.87 × 10	8.7	0.007 × 100
0.7	6.0023 × 100	600.23	0.496 × 1000	496	0.013 × 100
1.3	0.701 × 10	7.01	8.7 × 1000	8700	0.004 × 10
0.04	0.496 × 1000	496	1.09 × 100	109	0.85 × 10

Decimals: Ordering in Ascending Order

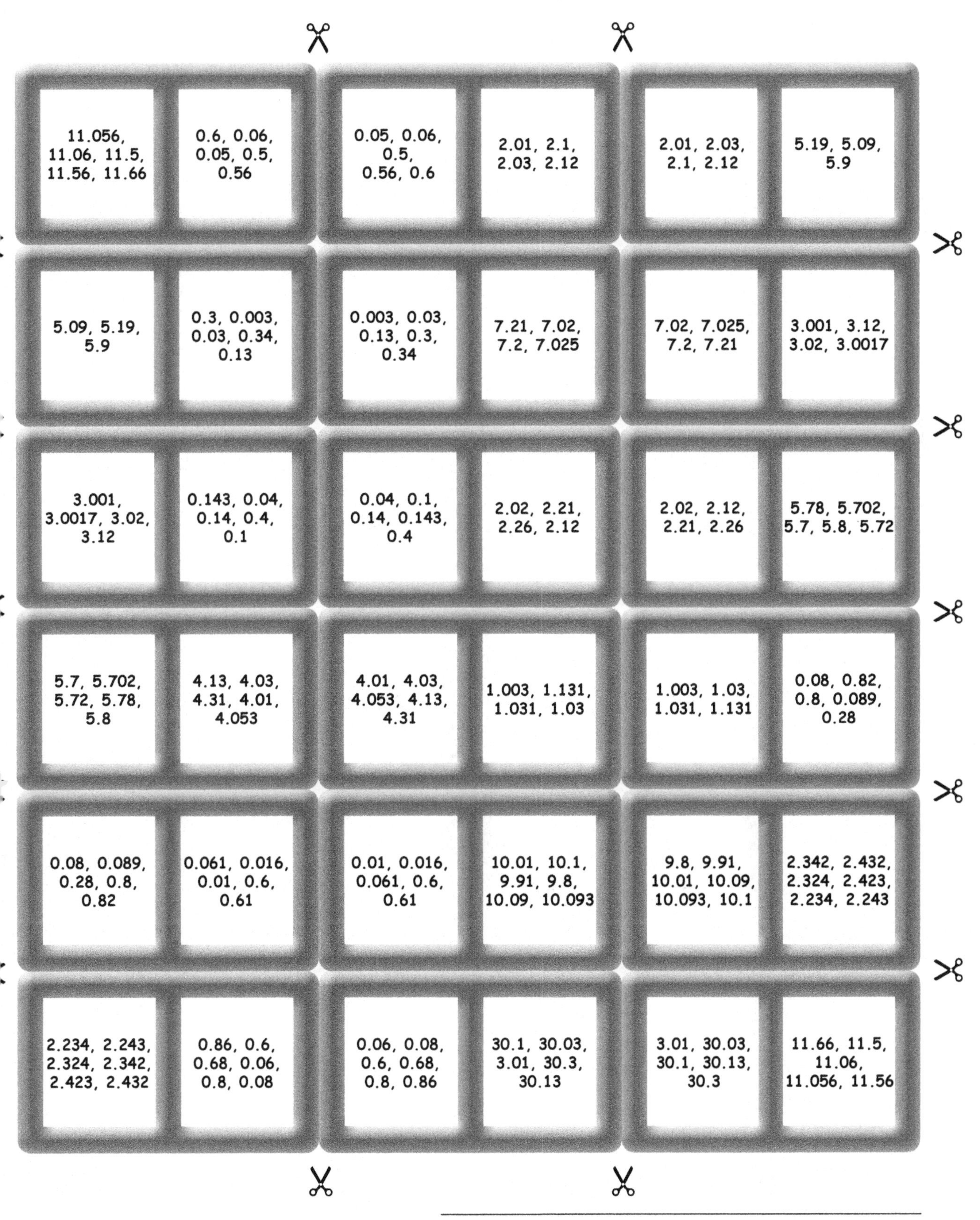

11.056, 11.06, 11.5, 11.56, 11.66	0.6, 0.06, 0.05, 0.5, 0.56	0.05, 0.06, 0.5, 0.56, 0.6	2.01, 2.1, 2.03, 2.12	2.01, 2.03, 2.1, 2.12	5.19, 5.09, 5.9
5.09, 5.19, 5.9	0.3, 0.003, 0.03, 0.34, 0.13	0.003, 0.03, 0.13, 0.3, 0.34	7.21, 7.02, 7.2, 7.025	7.02, 7.025, 7.2, 7.21	3.001, 3.12, 3.02, 3.0017
3.001, 3.0017, 3.02, 3.12	0.143, 0.04, 0.14, 0.4, 0.1	0.04, 0.1, 0.14, 0.143, 0.4	2.02, 2.21, 2.26, 2.12	2.02, 2.12, 2.21, 2.26	5.78, 5.702, 5.7, 5.8, 5.72
5.7, 5.702, 5.72, 5.78, 5.8	4.13, 4.03, 4.31, 4.01, 4.053	4.01, 4.03, 4.053, 4.13, 4.31	1.003, 1.131, 1.031, 1.03	1.003, 1.03, 1.031, 1.131	0.08, 0.82, 0.8, 0.089, 0.28
0.08, 0.089, 0.28, 0.8, 0.82	0.061, 0.016, 0.01, 0.6, 0.61	0.01, 0.016, 0.061, 0.6, 0.61	10.01, 10.1, 9.91, 9.8, 10.09, 10.093	9.8, 9.91, 10.01, 10.09, 10.093, 10.1	2.342, 2.432, 2.324, 2.423, 2.234, 2.243
2.234, 2.243, 2.324, 2.342, 2.423, 2.432	0.86, 0.6, 0.68, 0.06, 0.8, 0.08	0.06, 0.08, 0.6, 0.68, 0.8, 0.86	30.1, 30.03, 3.01, 30.3, 30.13	3.01, 30.03, 30.1, 30.13, 30.3	11.66, 11.5, 11.06, 11.056, 11.56

Divisibility by 3 Domino

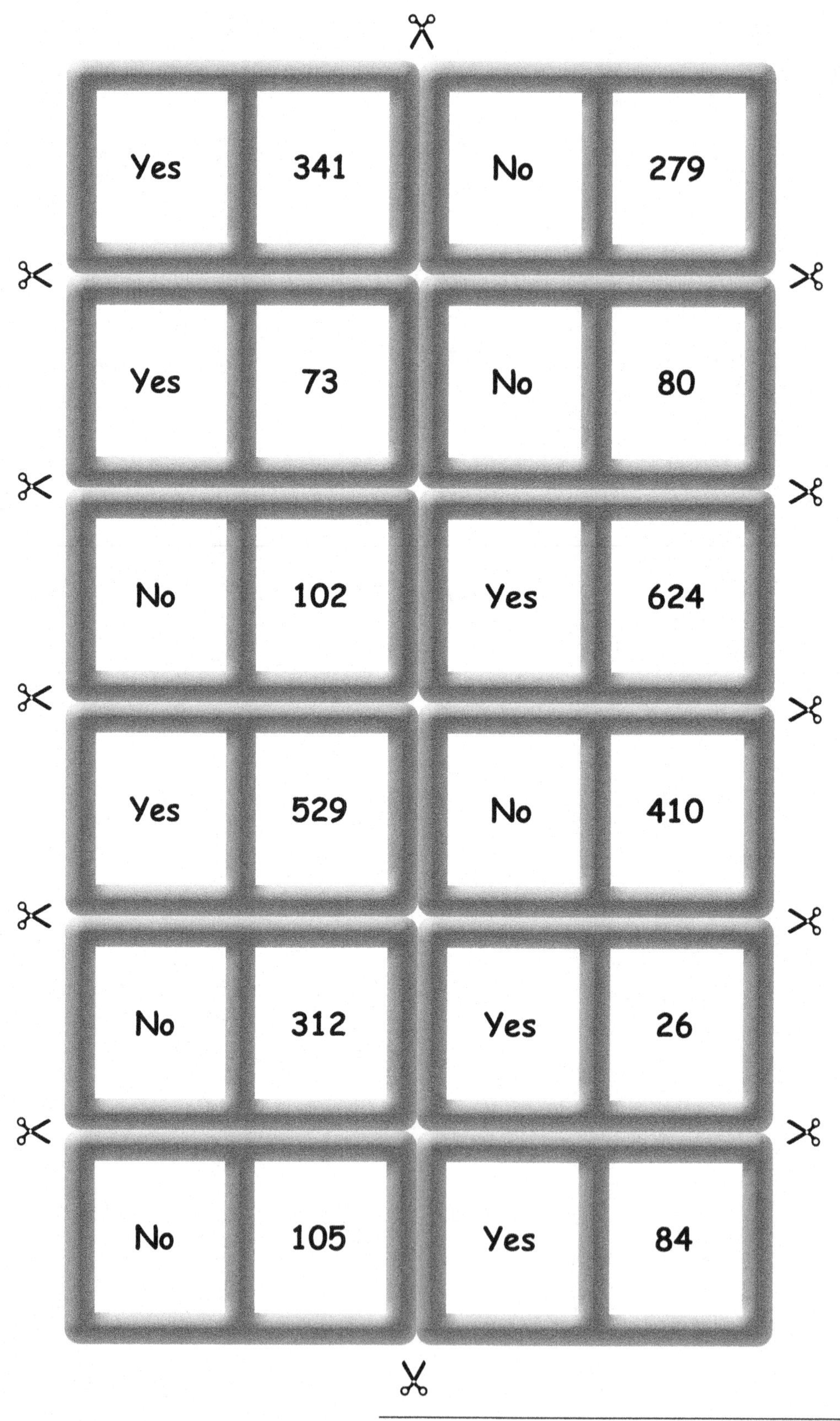

Yes	341	No	279
Yes	73	No	80
No	102	Yes	624
Yes	529	No	410
No	312	Yes	26
No	105	Yes	84

Division Dominoes: 2 digit by 1 digit

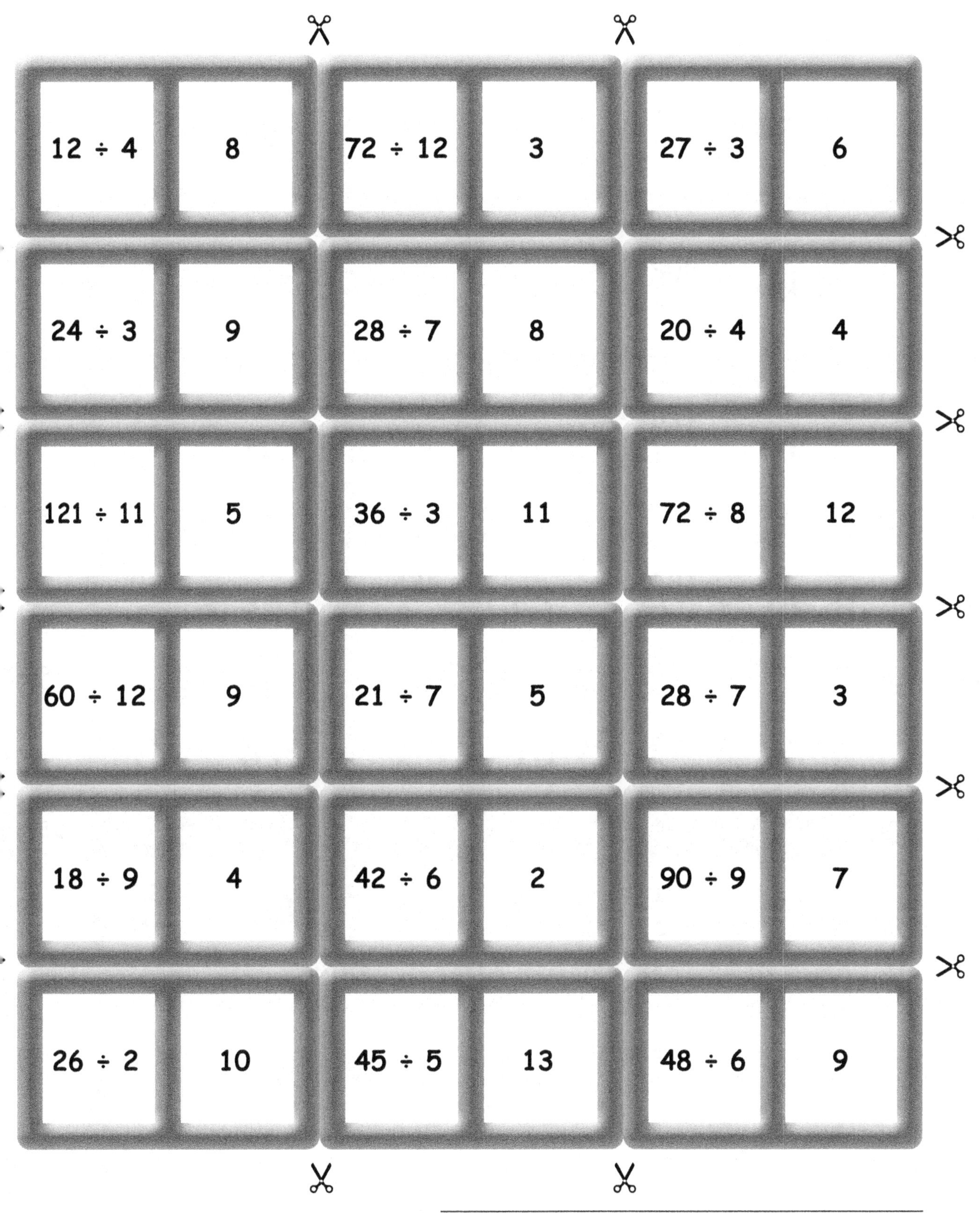

12 ÷ 4	8	72 ÷ 12	3	27 ÷ 3	6
24 ÷ 3	9	28 ÷ 7	8	20 ÷ 4	4
121 ÷ 11	5	36 ÷ 3	11	72 ÷ 8	12
60 ÷ 12	9	21 ÷ 7	5	28 ÷ 7	3
18 ÷ 9	4	42 ÷ 6	2	90 ÷ 9	7
26 ÷ 2	10	45 ÷ 5	13	48 ÷ 6	9

Division by 1 digit

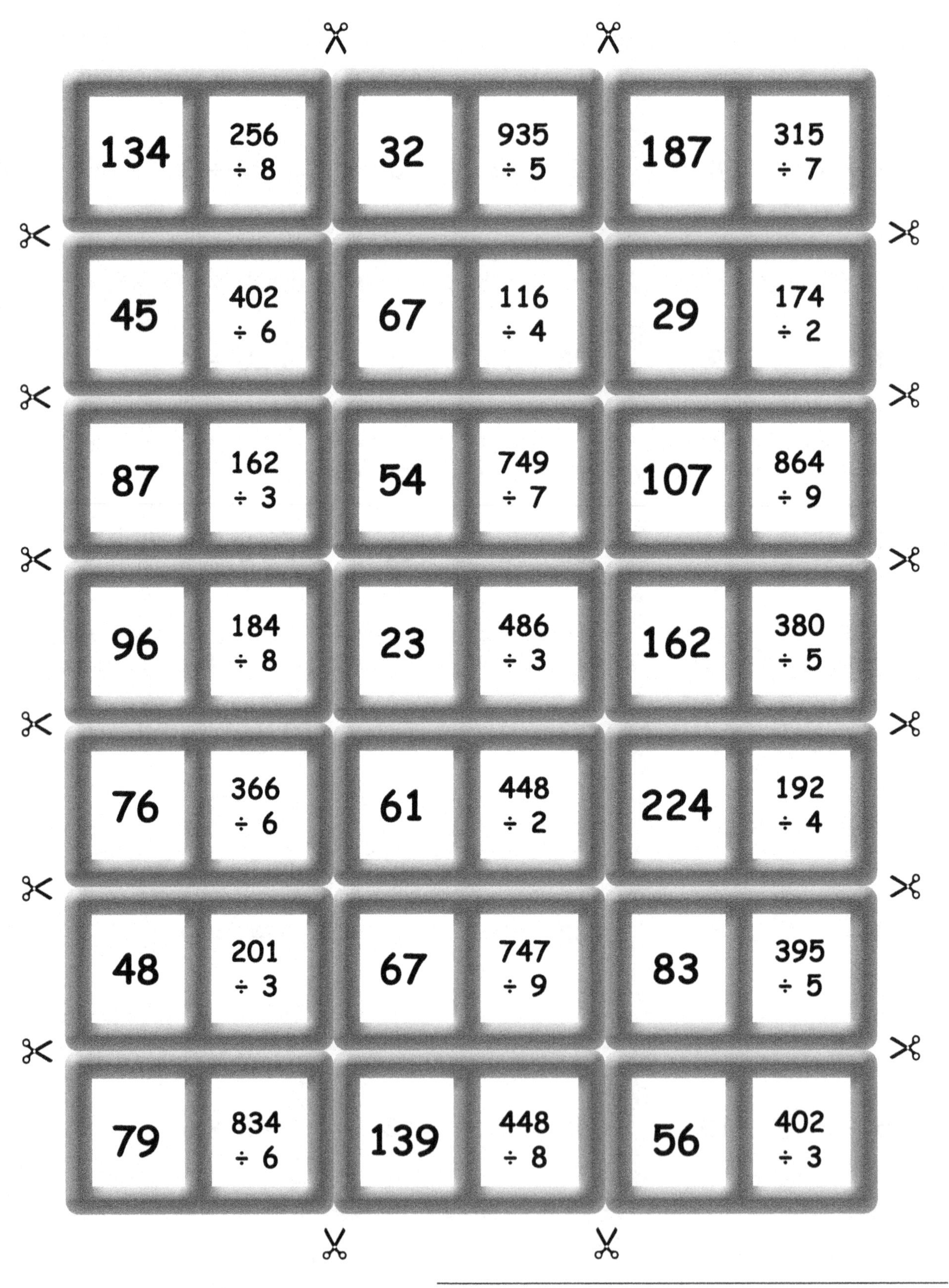

134	256 ÷ 8	**32**	935 ÷ 5	**187**	315 ÷ 7
45	402 ÷ 6	**67**	116 ÷ 4	**29**	174 ÷ 2
87	162 ÷ 3	**54**	749 ÷ 7	**107**	864 ÷ 9
96	184 ÷ 8	**23**	486 ÷ 3	**162**	380 ÷ 5
76	366 ÷ 6	**61**	448 ÷ 2	**224**	192 ÷ 4
48	201 ÷ 3	**67**	747 ÷ 9	**83**	395 ÷ 5
79	834 ÷ 6	**139**	448 ÷ 8	**56**	402 ÷ 3

Student Sheet

Doubling and Halving

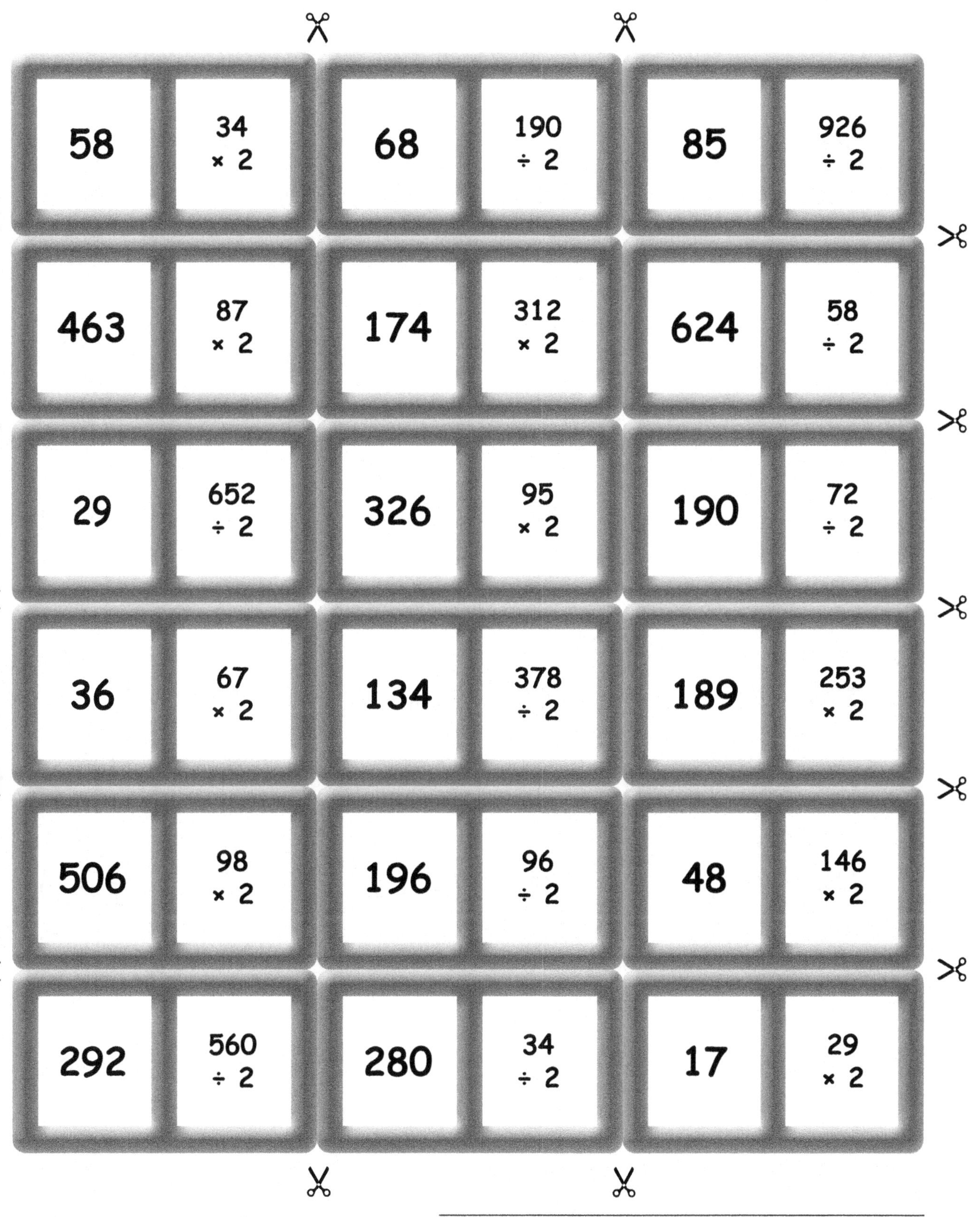

58	34 × 2	68	190 ÷ 2	85	926 ÷ 2
463	87 × 2	174	312 × 2	624	58 ÷ 2
29	652 ÷ 2	326	95 × 2	190	72 ÷ 2
36	67 × 2	134	378 ÷ 2	189	253 × 2
506	98 × 2	196	96 ÷ 2	48	146 × 2
292	560 ÷ 2	280	34 ÷ 2	17	29 × 2

Fractions of Amounts Dominoes

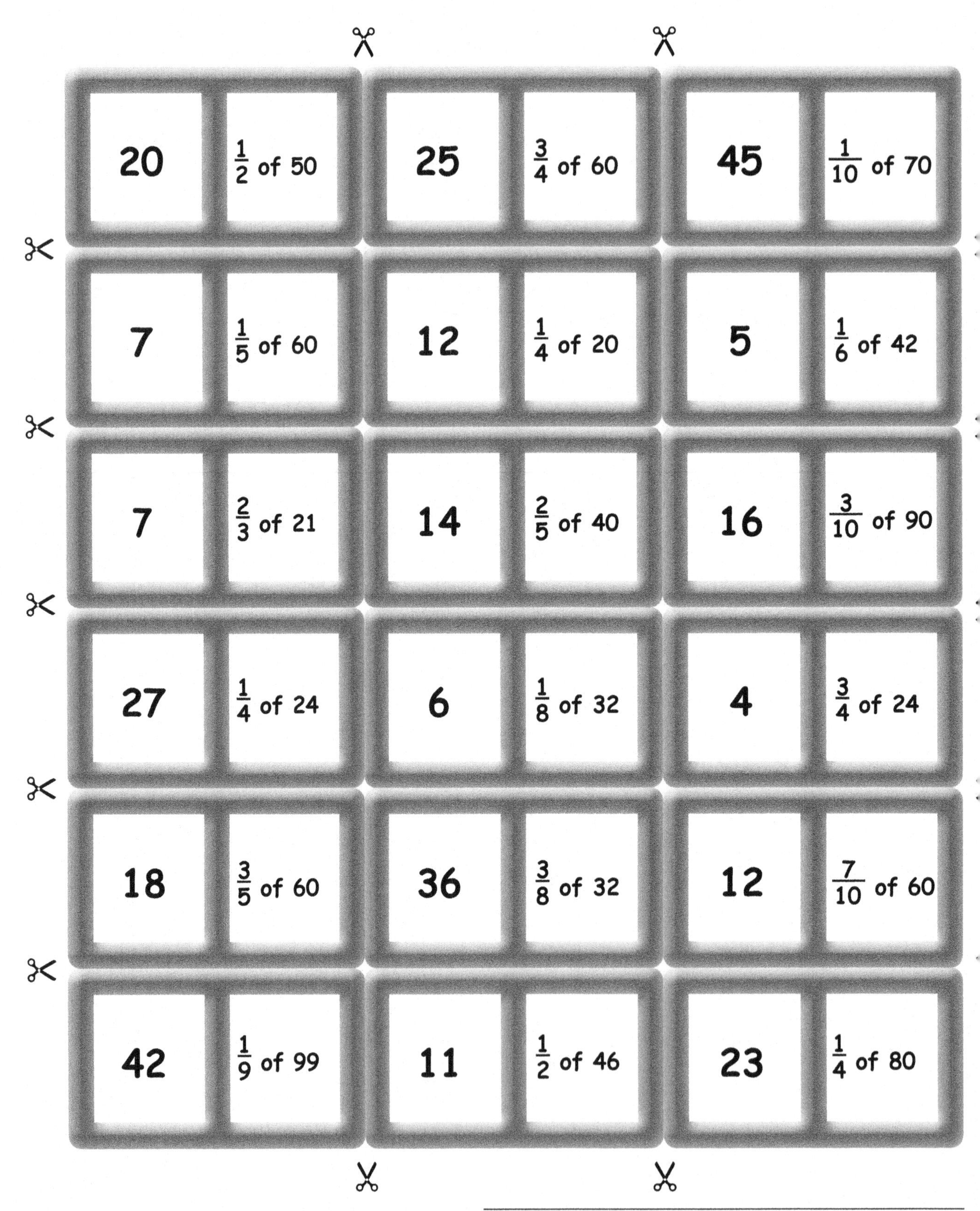

20	$\frac{1}{2}$ of 50	25	$\frac{3}{4}$ of 60	45	$\frac{1}{10}$ of 70
7	$\frac{1}{5}$ of 60	12	$\frac{1}{4}$ of 20	5	$\frac{1}{6}$ of 42
7	$\frac{2}{3}$ of 21	14	$\frac{2}{5}$ of 40	16	$\frac{3}{10}$ of 90
27	$\frac{1}{4}$ of 24	6	$\frac{1}{8}$ of 32	4	$\frac{3}{4}$ of 24
18	$\frac{3}{5}$ of 60	36	$\frac{3}{8}$ of 32	12	$\frac{7}{10}$ of 60
42	$\frac{1}{9}$ of 99	11	$\frac{1}{2}$ of 46	23	$\frac{1}{4}$ of 80

Equivalent Fractions Dominoes

$\frac{7}{35}$	$\frac{3}{4}$	$\frac{15}{20}$	$\frac{1}{2}$	$\frac{12}{24}$	$\frac{2}{5}$
$\frac{12}{30}$	$\frac{5}{6}$	$\frac{20}{24}$	$\frac{4}{9}$	$\frac{28}{63}$	$\frac{4}{5}$
$\frac{20}{25}$	$\frac{2}{3}$	$\frac{12}{18}$	$\frac{7}{8}$	$\frac{28}{32}$	$\frac{1}{4}$
$\frac{7}{28}$	$\frac{1}{6}$	$\frac{6}{36}$	$\frac{2}{9}$	$\frac{10}{45}$	$\frac{3}{10}$
$\frac{12}{40}$	$\frac{3}{8}$	$\frac{21}{56}$	$\frac{7}{9}$	$\frac{21}{27}$	$\frac{3}{5}$
$\frac{15}{25}$	$\frac{2}{11}$	$\frac{24}{132}$	$\frac{1}{3}$	$\frac{6}{18}$	$\frac{1}{5}$

Midpoints of Number Pairs

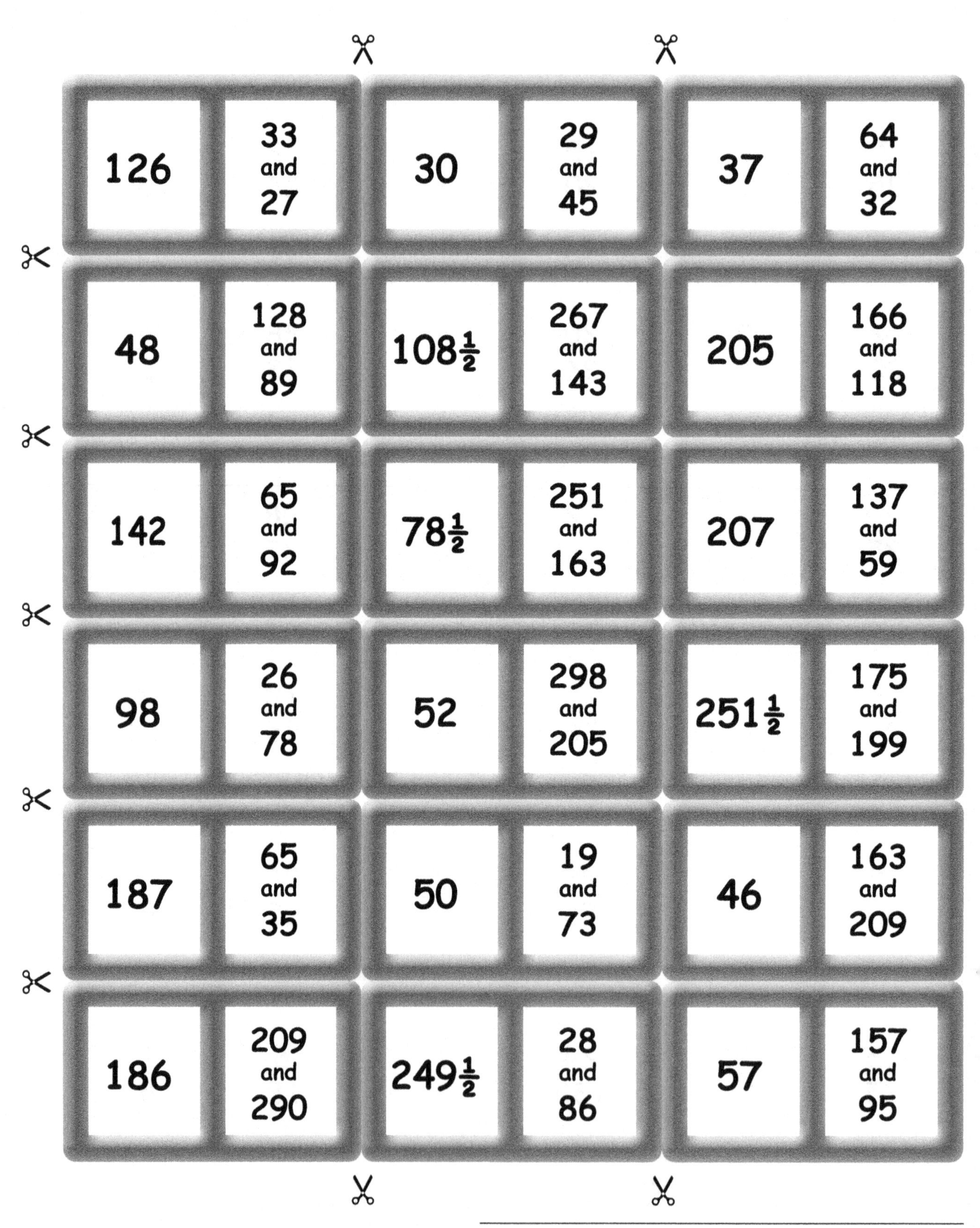

126	33 and 27	30	29 and 45	37	64 and 32
48	128 and 89	108½	267 and 143	205	166 and 118
142	65 and 92	78½	251 and 163	207	137 and 59
98	26 and 78	52	298 and 205	251½	175 and 199
187	65 and 35	50	19 and 73	46	163 and 209
186	209 and 290	249½	28 and 86	57	157 and 95

Money: Finding Totals

£4.02	£1.24 + £0.89	£2.13	56p + 32p	88p	£1.35 + 76p
£2.11	49p + 78p	£1.27	19p + 66p	85p	£3.41 + £5.02
£8.43	9p + 97p	£1.06	76p + 83p	£1.59	£6.07 + £0.99
£7.06	£9.97 + £2.99	£12.96	£8.21 + £1.55	£9.76	33p + 82p
£1.15	£0.43 + 26p	69p	£4.01 + £0.74	£4.75	96p + 56p
£1.52	£0.87 + £7.75	£8.62	93p + 29p	£1.22	£0.75 + £3.27

Money: Giving Change

£1.37	£2 – 50p	£1.50	£10 – £4.45	£5.55	£5 – £3.14
£1.86	£1 – 57p	£0.43	£2 – £0.79	£1.21	£2 – 92p
£1.08	£1 – £0.48	52p	£5 – £2.23	£2.77	£2 – 14p
£1.86	£5 – £4.06	£0.94	£2 – 3p	£1.97	£10 – £3.30
£6.70	£1 – 81p	£0.19	£2 – 26p	£1.74	£5 – £2.15
£2.85	£1 – 98p	£0.02	£5 – £0.60	£4.40	£2 – 63p

Tables Dominoes

18	3 X 4		12	7 X 5		35	6 X 9
54	2 X 5		10	8 X 6		48	7 X 4
28	3 X 7		21	9 X 8		72	4 X 9
36	10 X 3		30	11 X 5		55	12 X 7
84	7 X 9		63	8 X 3		24	6 X 4
24	8 X 8		64	5 X 5		25	3 X 6

Multiplication Dominoes:
2 digit BY 1 digit

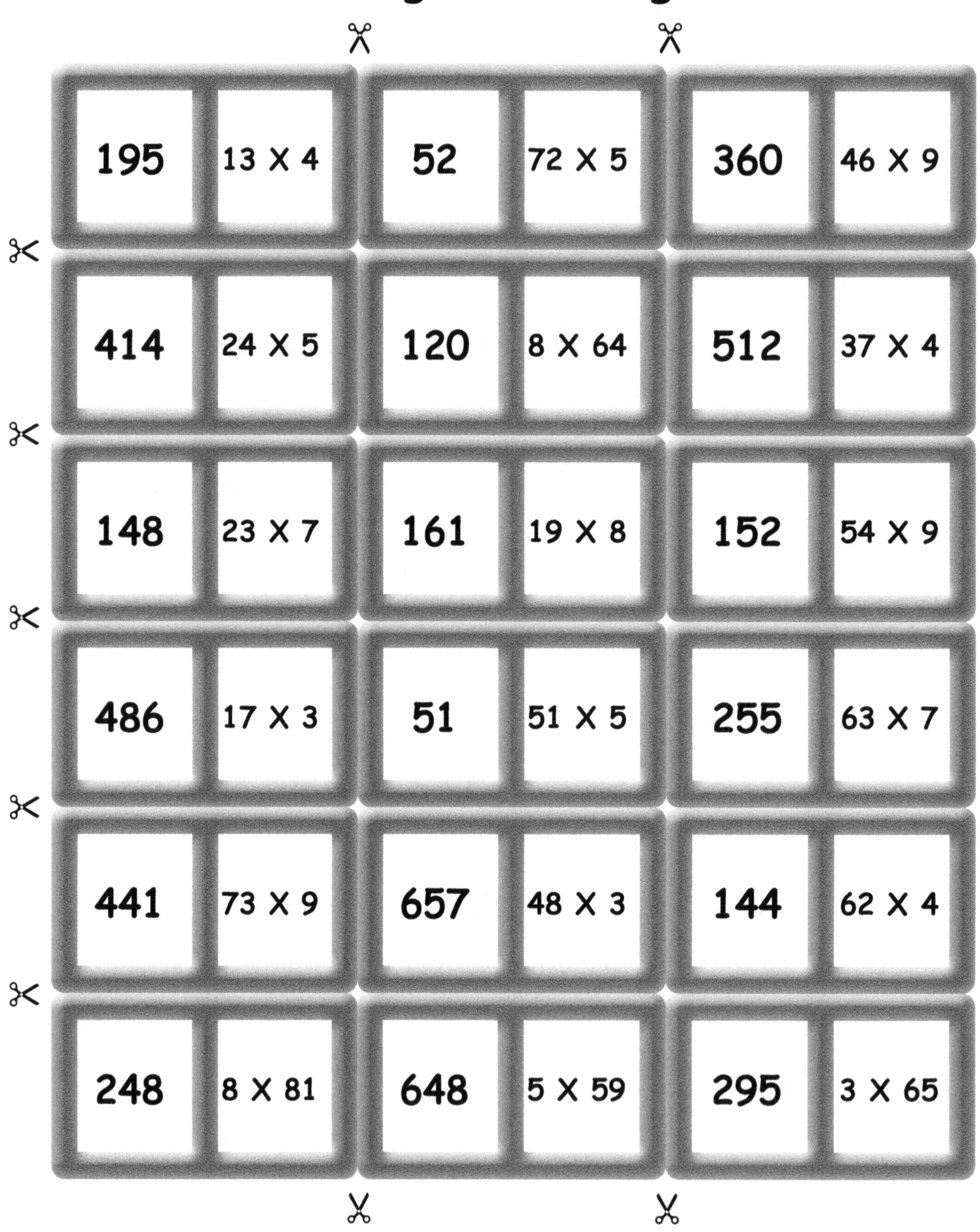

195	13 X 4	52	72 X 5	360	46 X 9
414	24 X 5	120	8 X 64	512	37 X 4
148	23 X 7	161	19 X 8	152	54 X 9
486	17 X 3	51	51 X 5	255	63 X 7
441	73 X 9	657	48 X 3	144	62 X 4
248	8 X 81	648	5 X 59	295	3 X 65

Highest Common Factor Dominoes

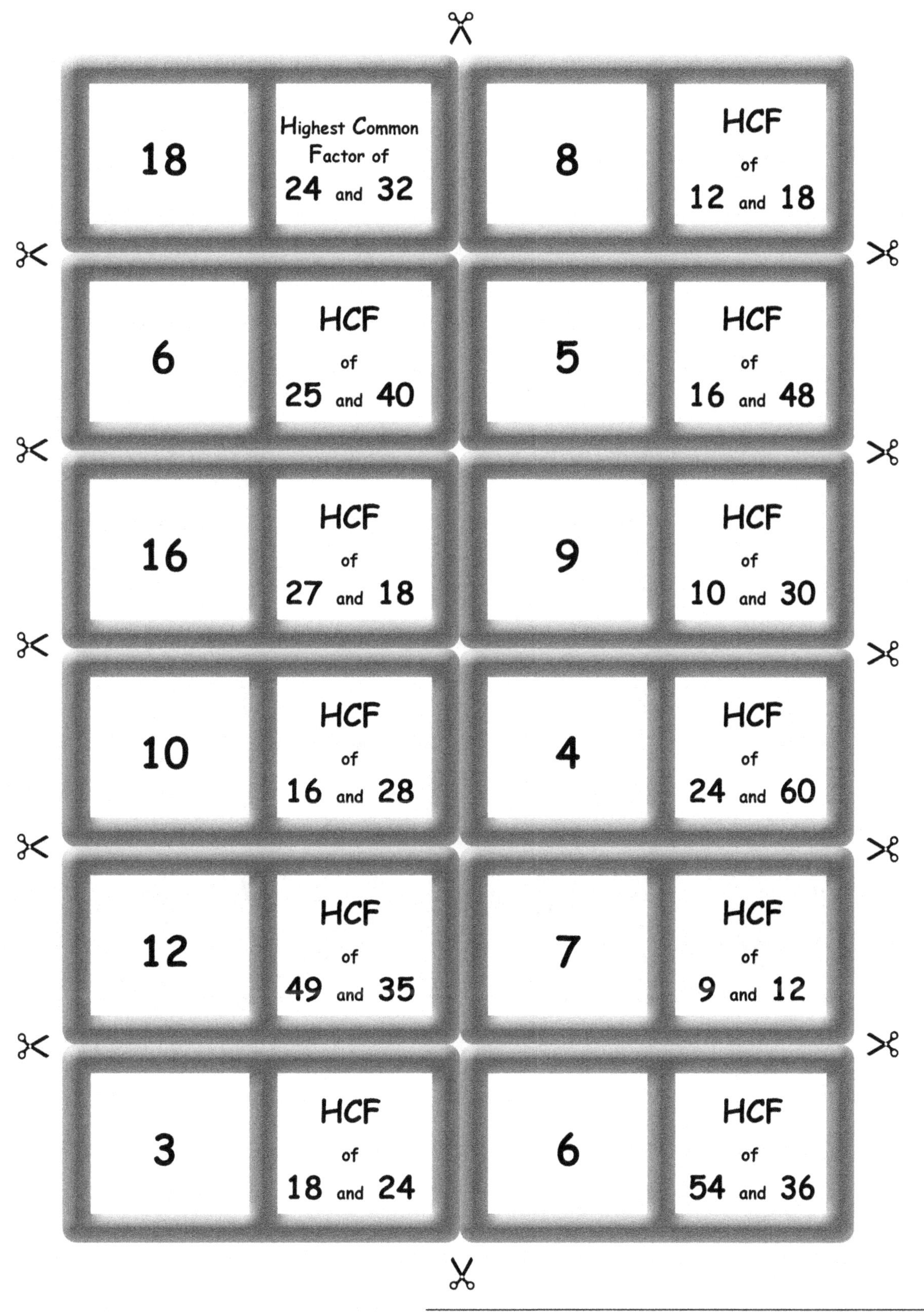

18	Highest Common Factor of 24 and 32	8	HCF of 12 and 18
6	HCF of 25 and 40	5	HCF of 16 and 48
16	HCF of 27 and 18	9	HCF of 10 and 30
10	HCF of 16 and 28	4	HCF of 24 and 60
12	HCF of 49 and 35	7	HCF of 9 and 12
3	HCF of 18 and 24	6	HCF of 54 and 36

Lowest Common Multiple Dominoes

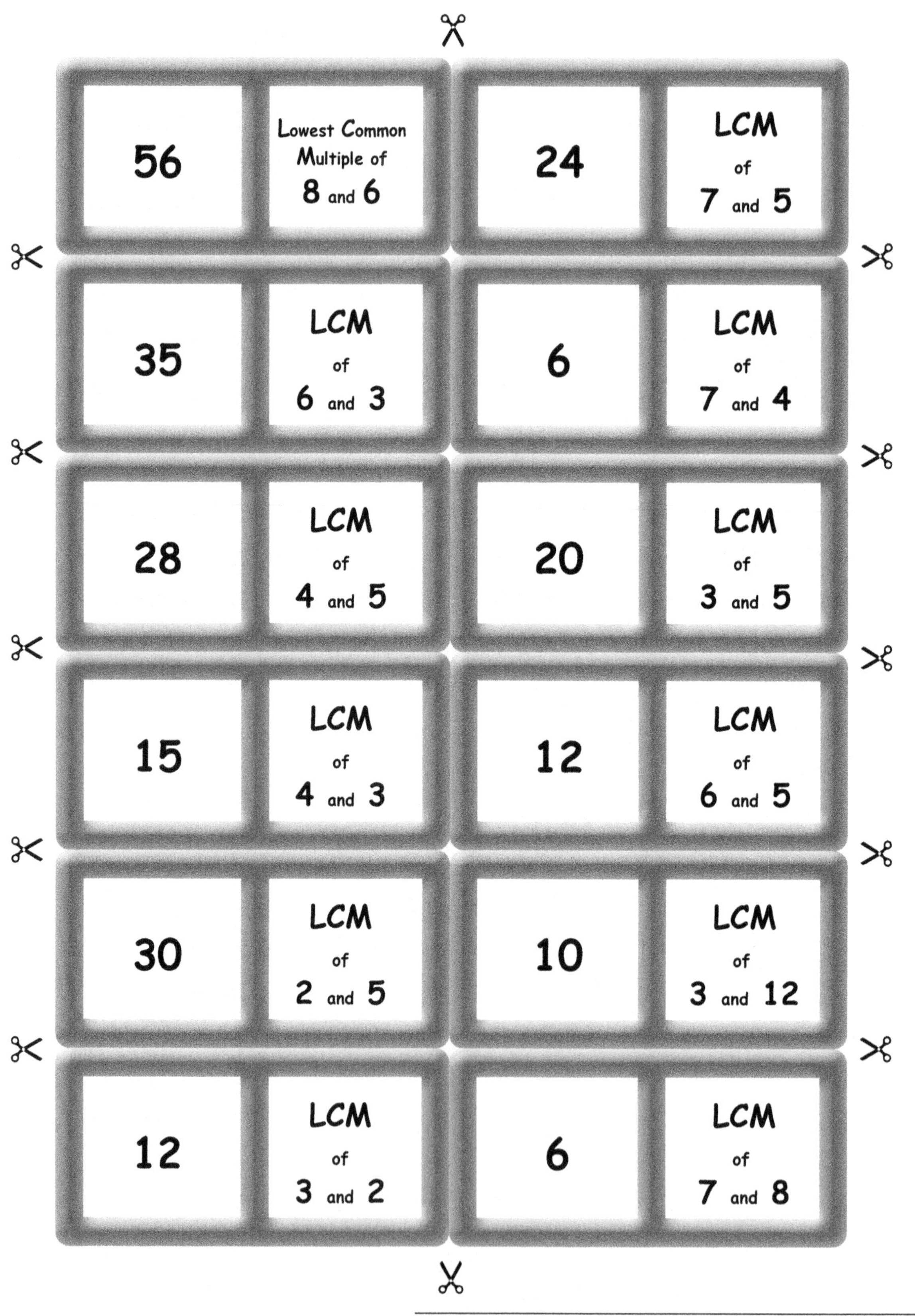

Simple Percentages Dominoes

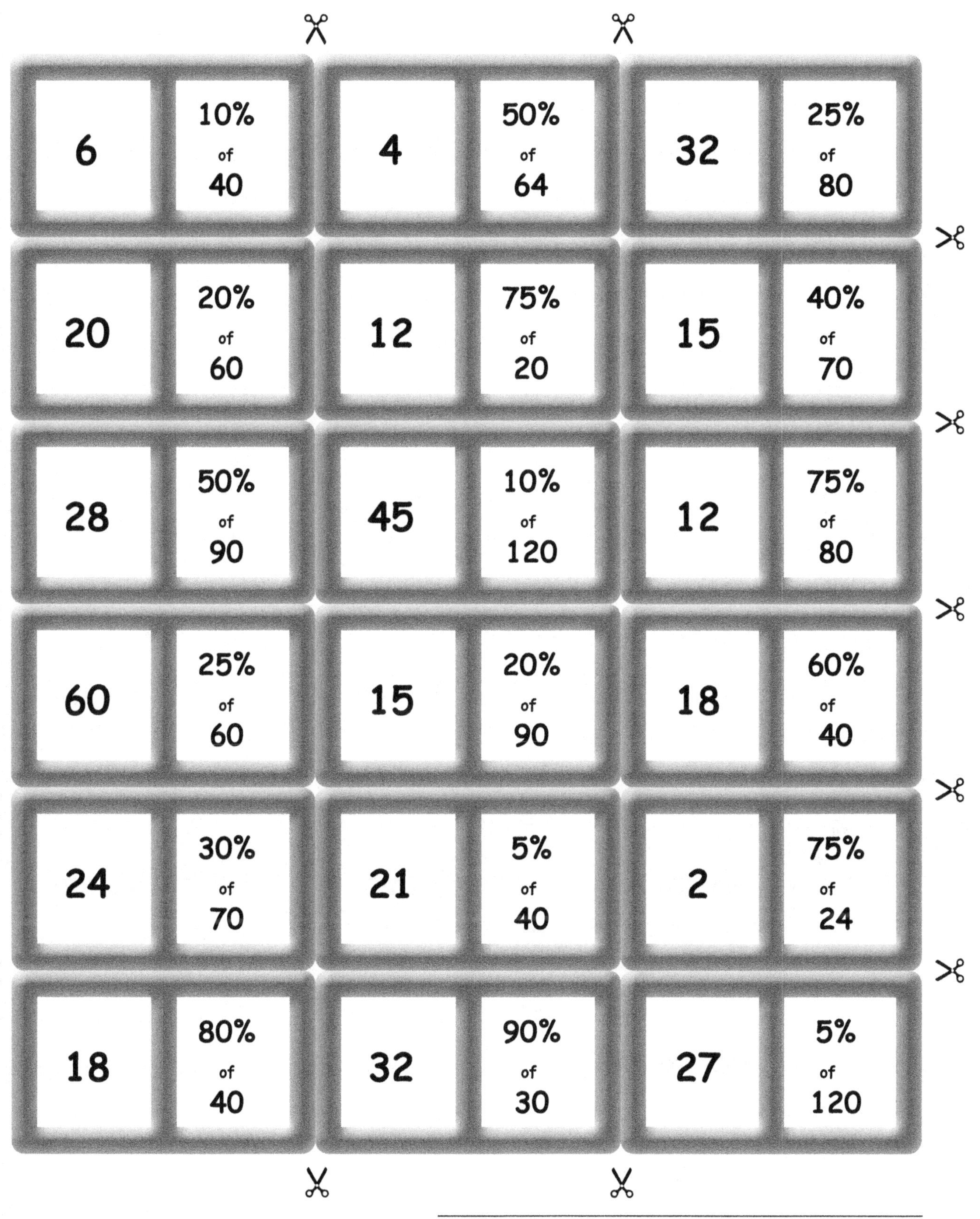

6	10% of 40	4	50% of 64	32	25% of 80
20	20% of 60	12	75% of 20	15	40% of 70
28	50% of 90	45	10% of 120	12	75% of 80
60	25% of 60	15	20% of 90	18	60% of 40
24	30% of 70	21	5% of 40	2	75% of 24
18	80% of 40	32	90% of 30	27	5% of 120

Perimeter with Numbers

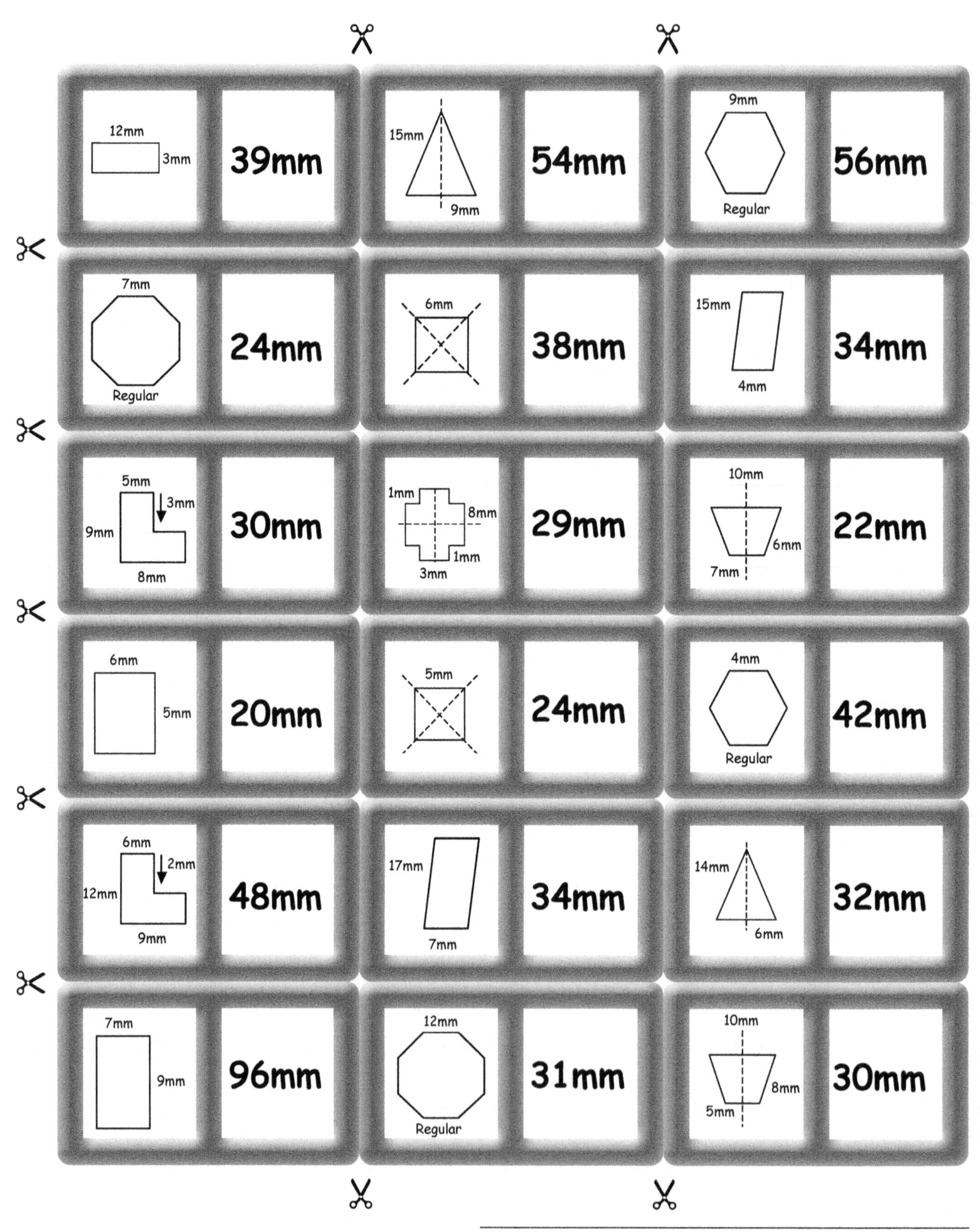

Round to Nearest Integer

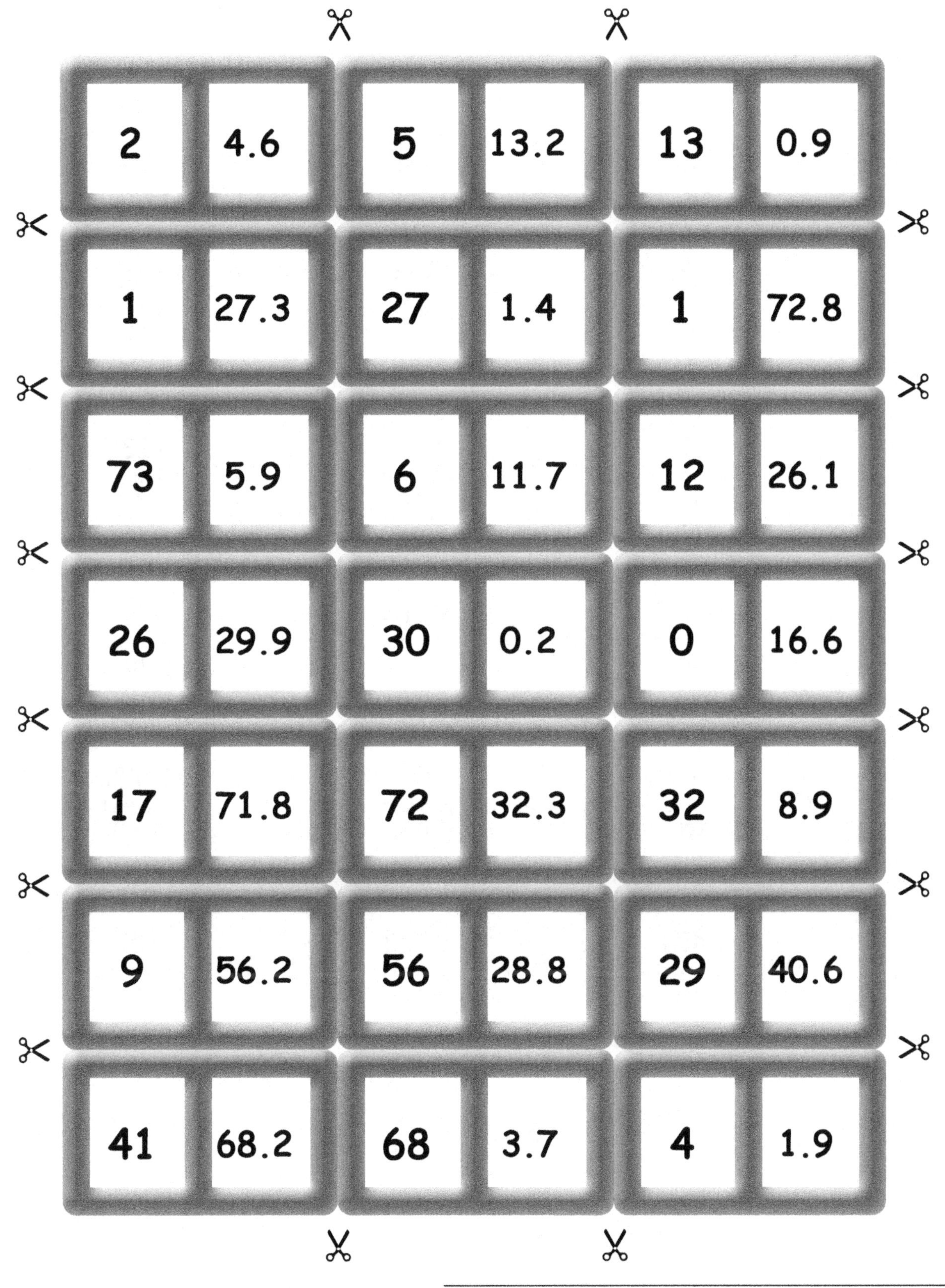

2 4.6	5 13.2	13 0.9
1 27.3	27 1.4	1 72.8
73 5.9	6 11.7	12 26.1
26 29.9	30 0.2	0 16.6
17 71.8	72 32.3	32 8.9
9 56.2	56 28.8	29 40.6
41 68.2	68 3.7	4 1.9

Round to Nearest Power of 10

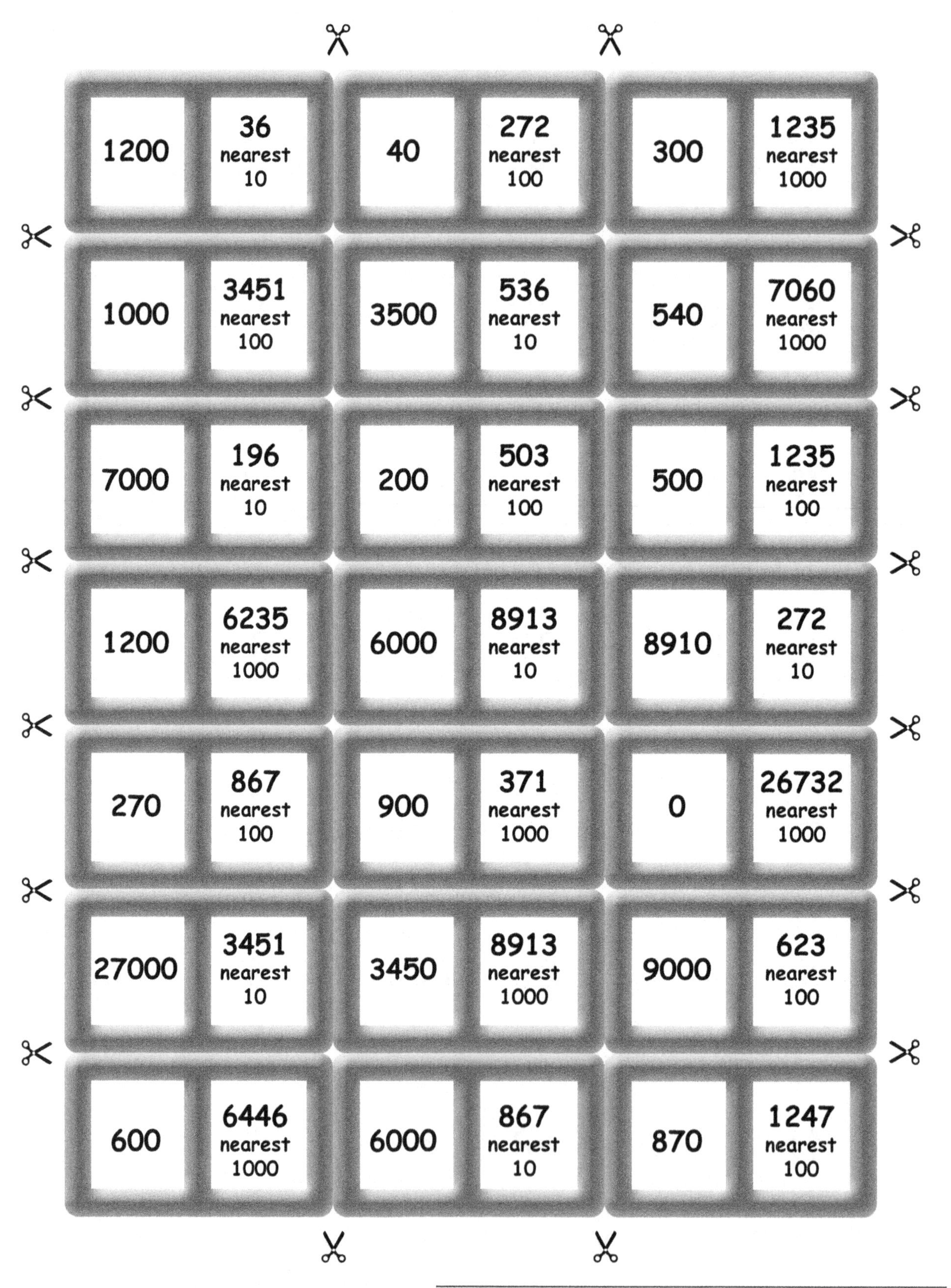

1200	36 nearest 10	40	272 nearest 100	300	1235 nearest 1000
1000	3451 nearest 100	3500	536 nearest 10	540	7060 nearest 1000
7000	196 nearest 10	200	503 nearest 100	500	1235 nearest 100
1200	6235 nearest 1000	6000	8913 nearest 10	8910	272 nearest 10
270	867 nearest 100	900	371 nearest 1000	0	26732 nearest 1000
27000	3451 nearest 10	3450	8913 nearest 1000	9000	623 nearest 100
600	6446 nearest 1000	6000	867 nearest 10	870	1247 nearest 100

Sequences to Find the Missing Rules

÷ 10	3, 5, 7, 9	+ 2	1, 3, 9, 27	× 3	2, 4, 8, 16
× 2	23, 15, 7, -1	- 8	6, 11, 16, 21	+ 5	20, 10, 5, 2½
÷ 2	19, 13, 7, 1	- 6	2, 10, 50, 250	× 5	19, 22, 25, 28
+ 3	3, 12, 48, 192	× 4	73, 69, 65, 61	- 4	23, 16, 9, 2
- 7	-4, -1, 2, 5	+ 3	0.3, 3, 30, 300	× 10	35, 24, 13, 2
- 11	6, 54, 486	× 9	8, 15, 22, 29	+ 7	900, 90, 9, 0.9

Sequences to Find the Missing Number

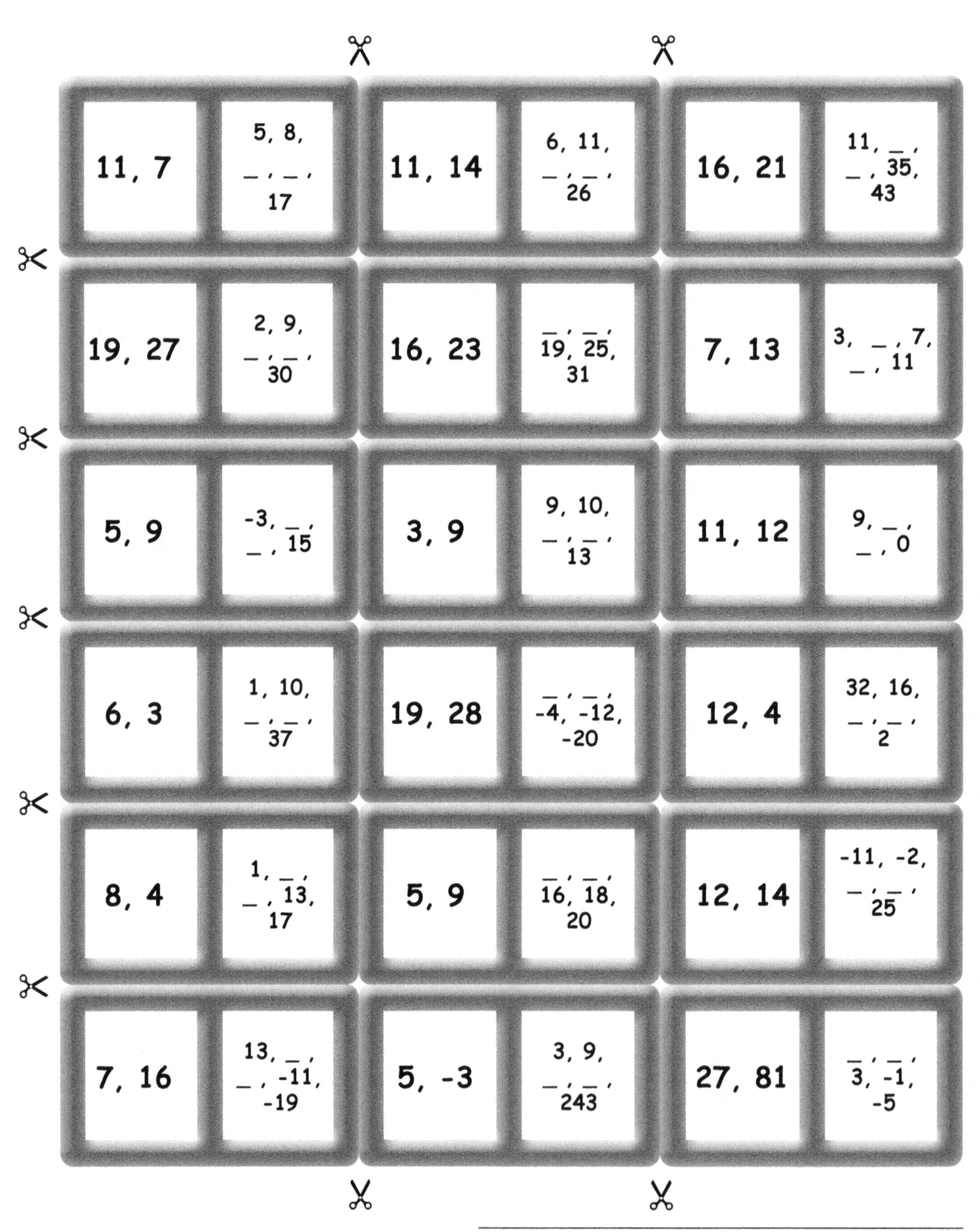

11, 7	5, 8, __ , __ , 17	**11, 14**	6, 11, __ , __ , 26	**16, 21**	11, __ , $\overline{35}$, 43
19, 27	2, 9, __ , __ , 30	**16, 23**	$\overline{19}$, $\overline{25}$, 31	**7, 13**	3, __ , 7, __ , 11
5, 9	-3, __ , $\overline{15}$	**3, 9**	9, 10, __ , __ , 13	**11, 12**	9, __ , 0
6, 3	1, 10, __ , __ , 37	**19, 28**	$\overline{-4}$, $\overline{-12}$, -20	**12, 4**	32, 16, __ , __ , 2
8, 4	1, __ , __ , 13, 17	**5, 9**	$\overline{16}$, $\overline{18}$, 20	**12, 14**	-11, -2, __ , __ , 25
7, 16	13, __ , __ , -11, -19	**5, -3**	3, 9, __ , __ , 243	**27, 81**	$\overline{3}$, $\overline{-1}$, -5

Subtraction Dominoes:
1 digit from 2 digits

13 - 4	15	24 - 9	64	72 - 8	32
39 - 7	56	64 - 8	16	23 - 7	28
35 - 7	7	16 - 9	47	56 - 9	63
71 - 8	46	54 - 8	86	92 - 6	33
40 - 7	39	44 - 5	3	11 - 8	35
41 - 6	85	93 - 8	48	55 - 7	9

Subtraction Dominoes: 2 digit from 2 digits

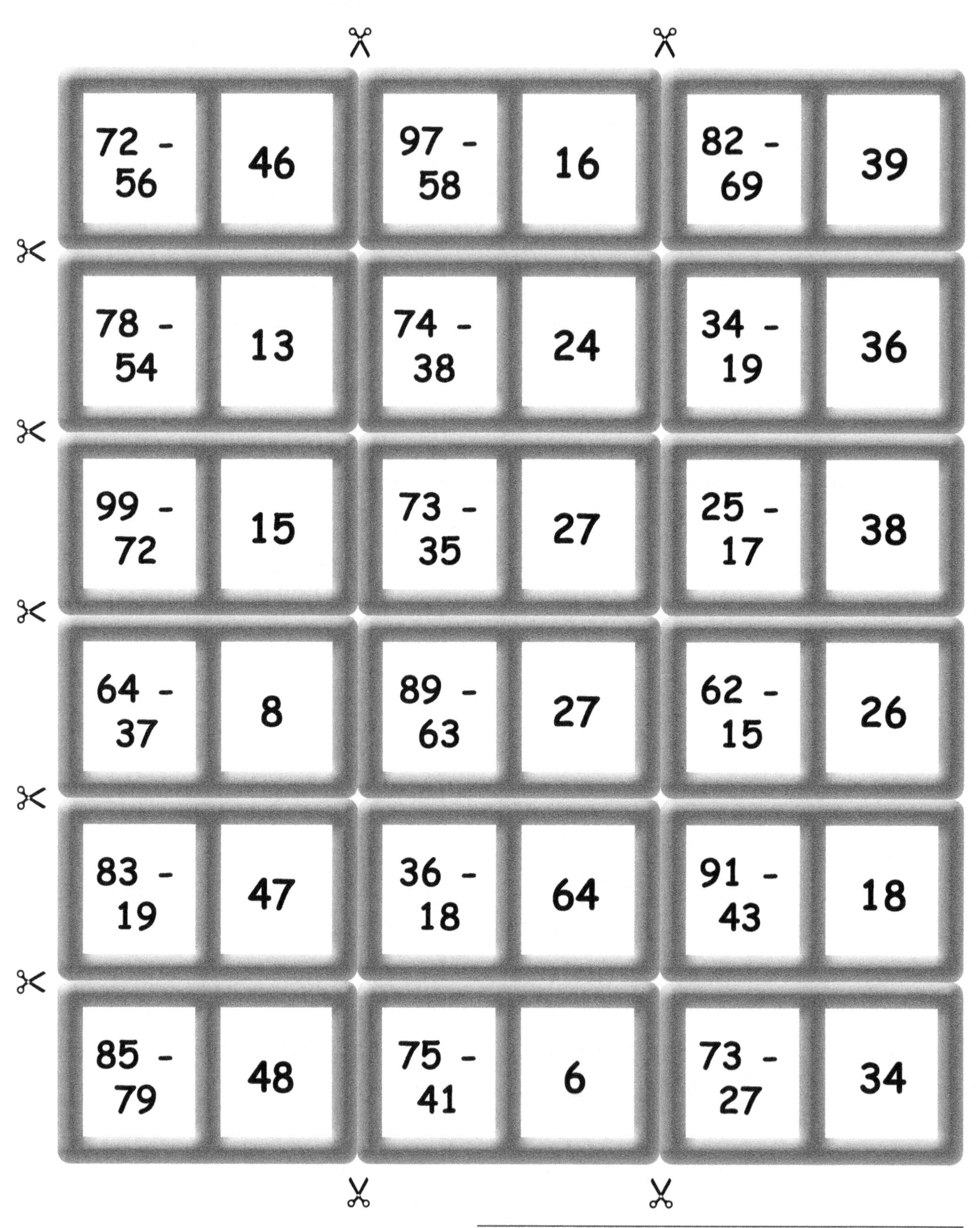

72 - 56	46	97 - 58	16	82 - 69	39
78 - 54	13	74 - 38	24	34 - 19	36
99 - 72	15	73 - 35	27	25 - 17	38
64 - 37	8	89 - 63	27	62 - 15	26
83 - 19	47	36 - 18	64	91 - 43	18
85 - 79	48	75 - 41	6	73 - 27	34

Subtraction Dominoes:
2 digits from 3 digits

412 – 56	194	572 – 98	356	621 – 84	474
738 – 54	537	734 – 78	684	190 – 34	656
572 – 29	156	435 – 73	543	253 – 78	362
372 – 64	175	895 – 63	308	125 – 62	832
819 – 63	63	738 – 76	756	291 – 43	662
709 – 85	248	675 – 47	624	267 – 73	628

Subtraction: 3 digits from 3 digits

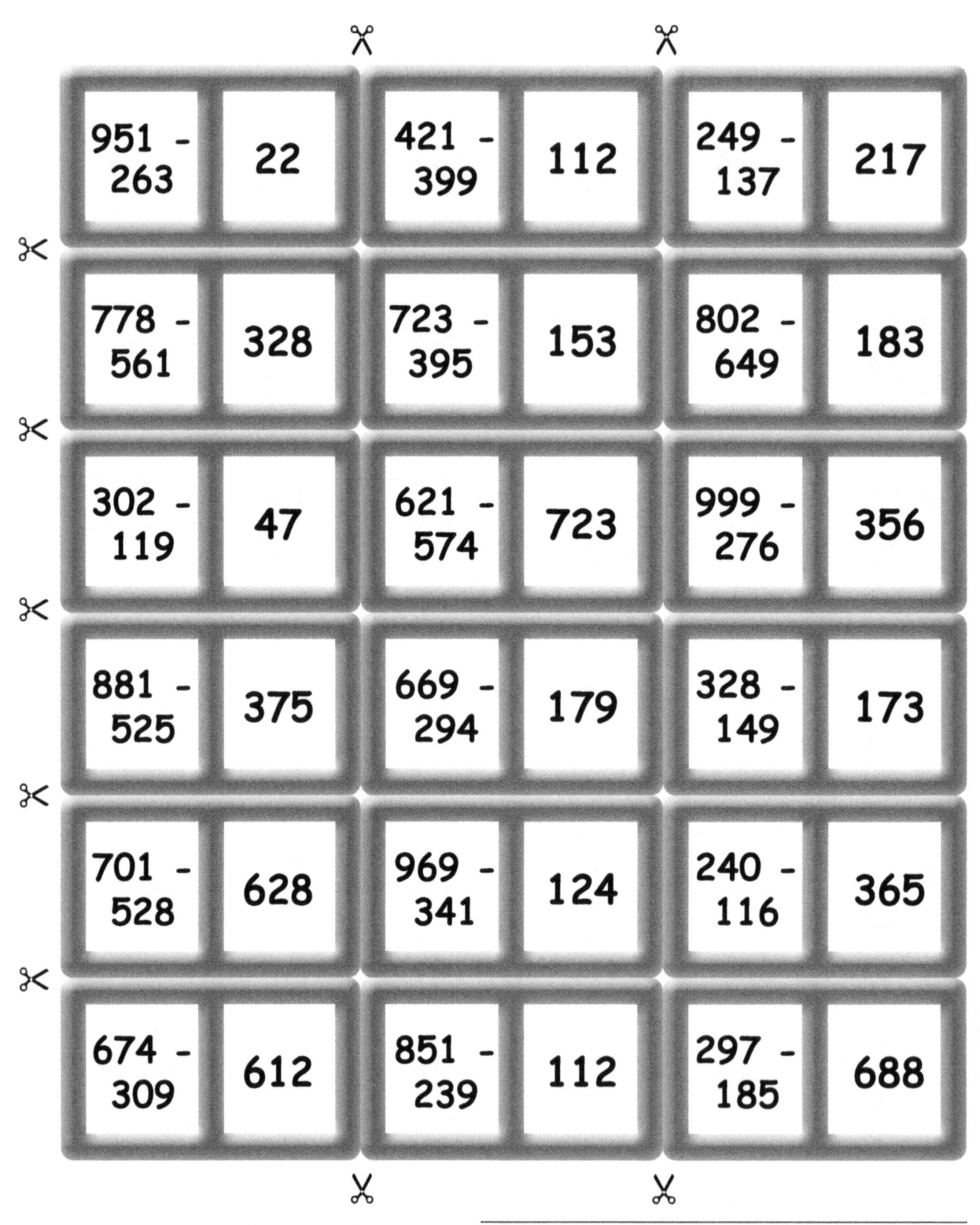

951 − 263	22	421 − 399	112	249 − 137	217
778 − 561	328	723 − 395	153	802 − 649	183
302 − 119	47	621 − 574	723	999 − 276	356
881 − 525	375	669 − 294	179	328 − 149	173
701 − 528	628	969 − 341	124	240 − 116	365
674 − 309	612	851 − 239	112	297 − 185	688

Time Dominoes

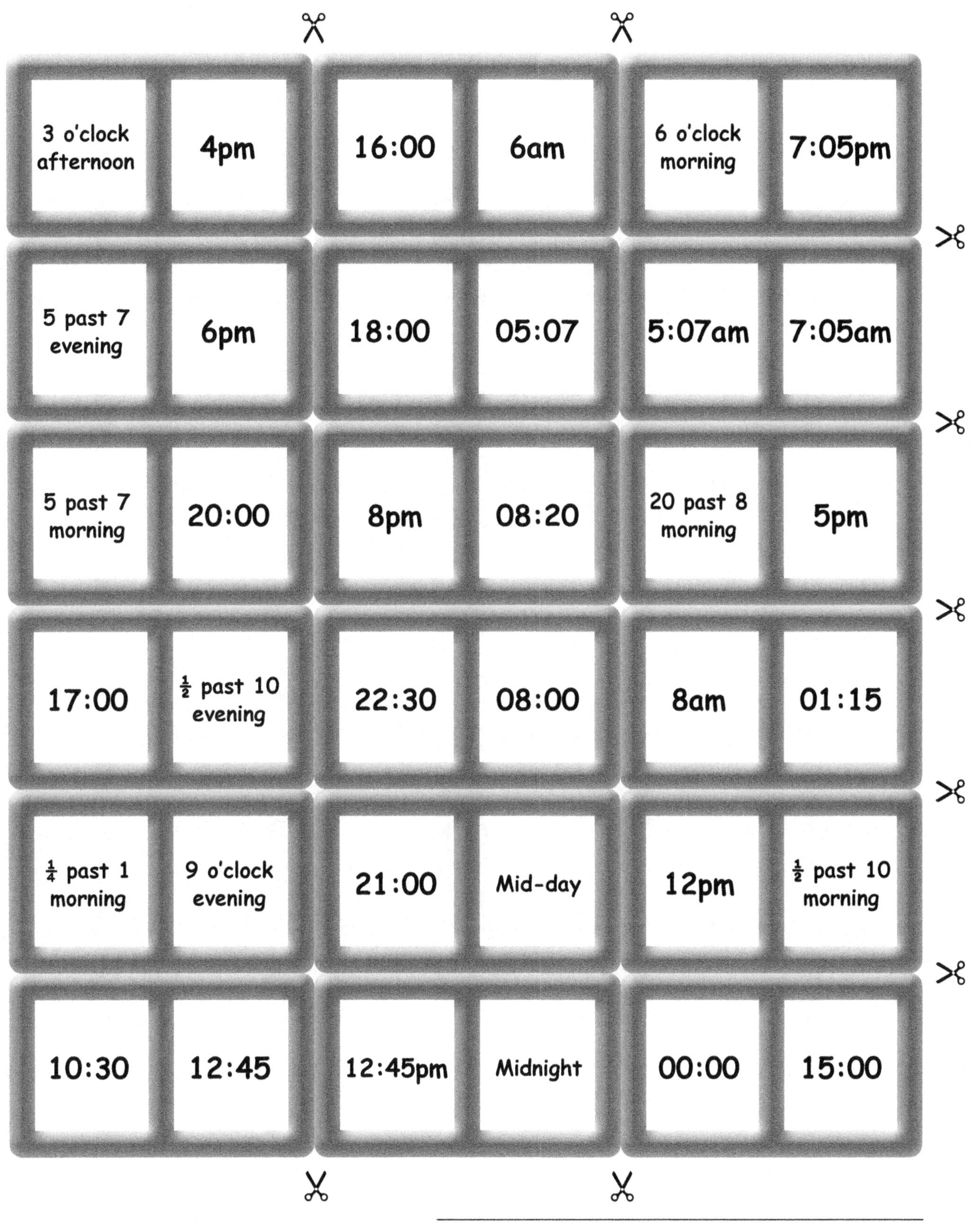

3 o'clock afternoon	4pm	16:00	6am	6 o'clock morning	7:05pm
5 past 7 evening	6pm	18:00	05:07	5:07am	7:05am
5 past 7 morning	20:00	8pm	08:20	20 past 8 morning	5pm
17:00	½ past 10 evening	22:30	08:00	8am	01:15
¼ past 1 morning	9 o'clock evening	21:00	Mid-day	12pm	½ past 10 morning
10:30	12:45	12:45pm	Midnight	00:00	15:00

Template for 10 Dominoes

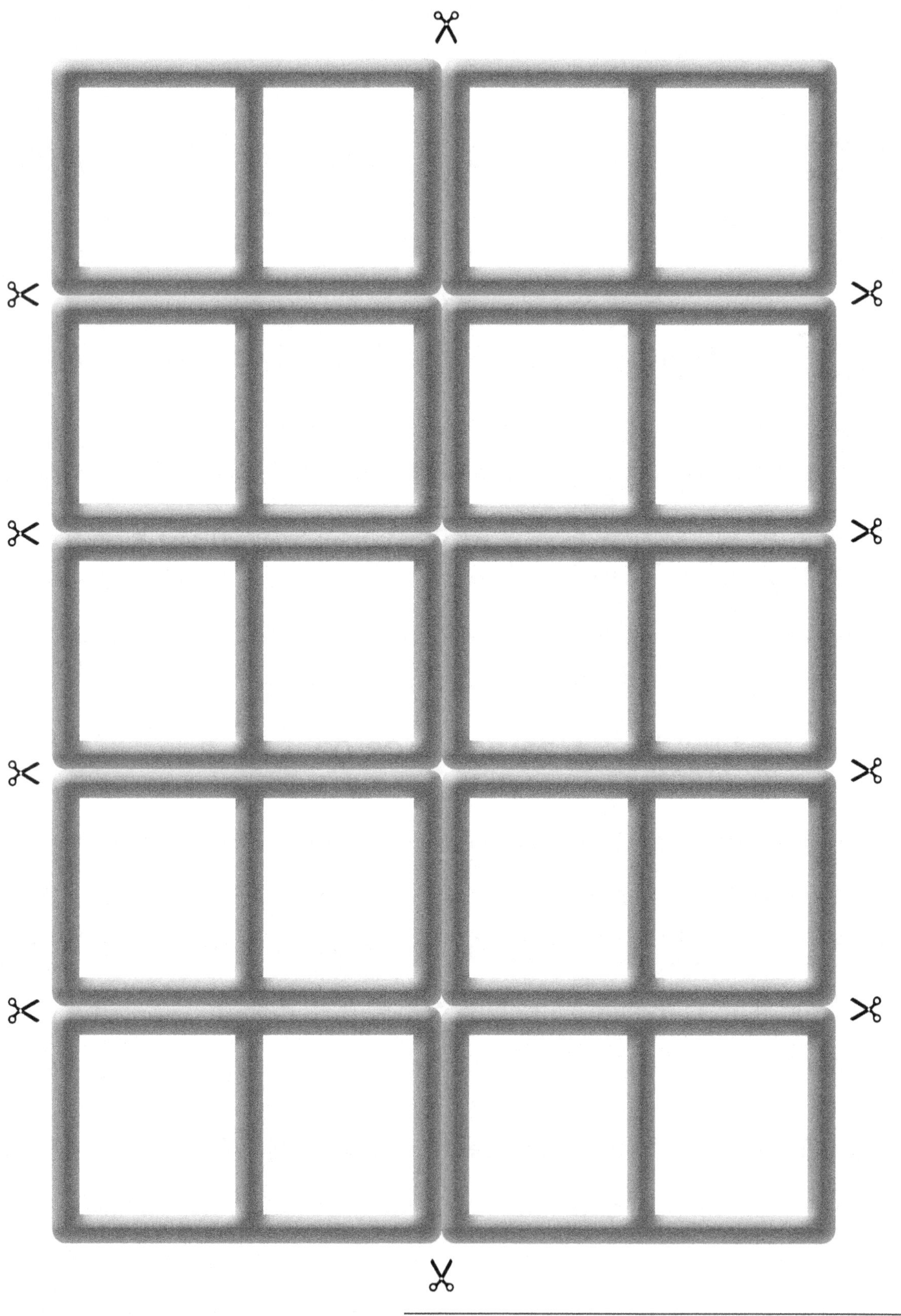

Template for 12 Dominoes

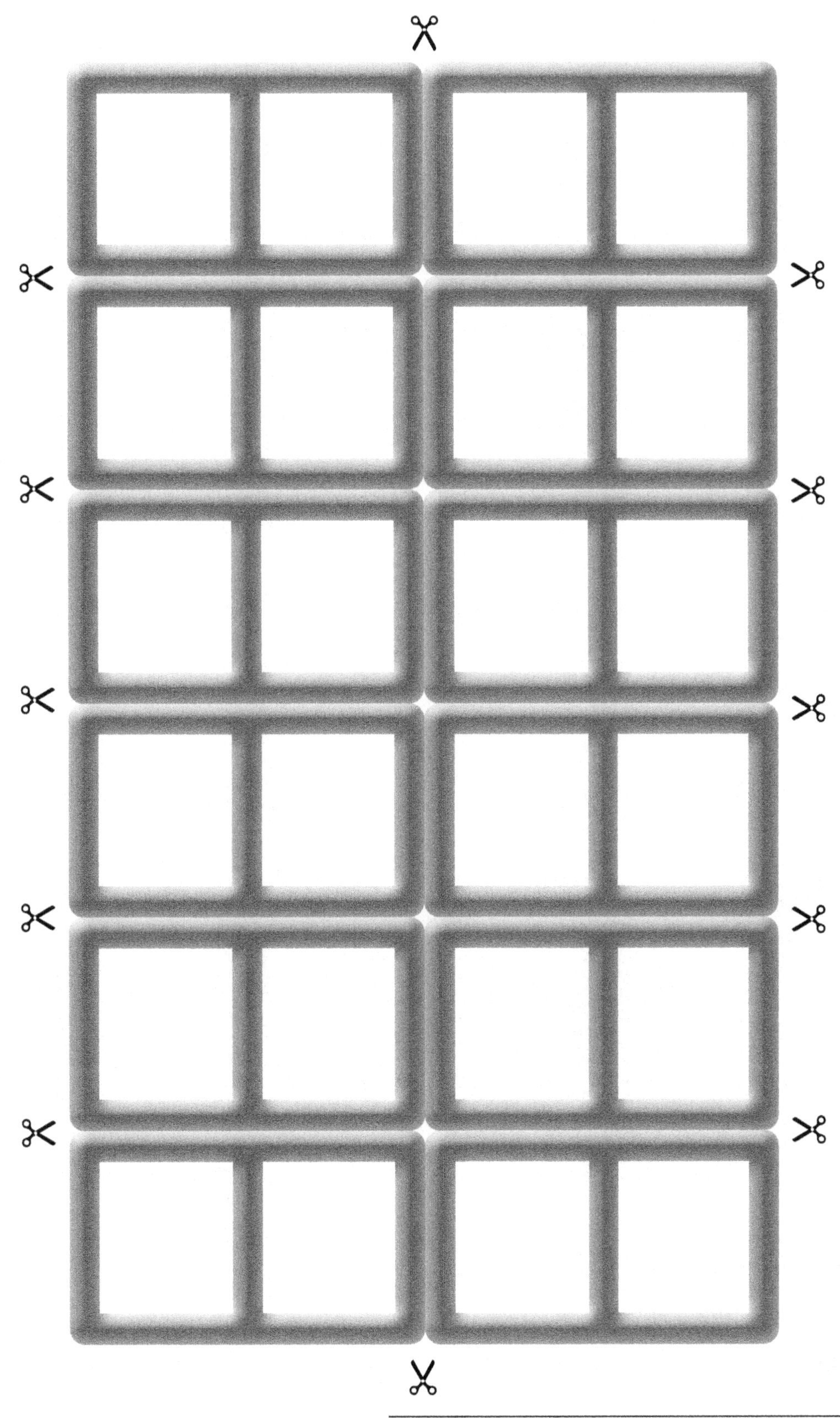

Template for 18 Dominoes

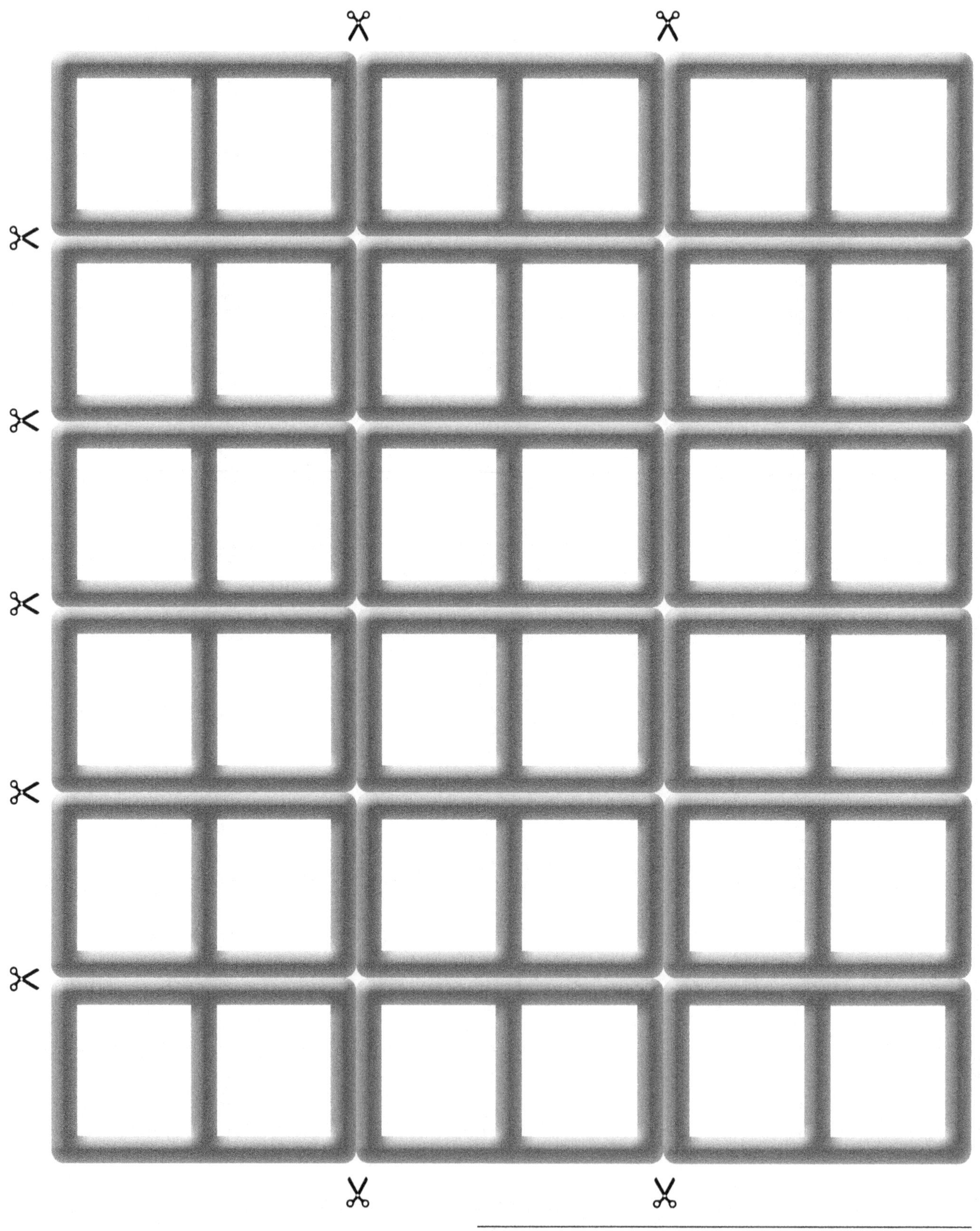

Template for 21 Dominoes

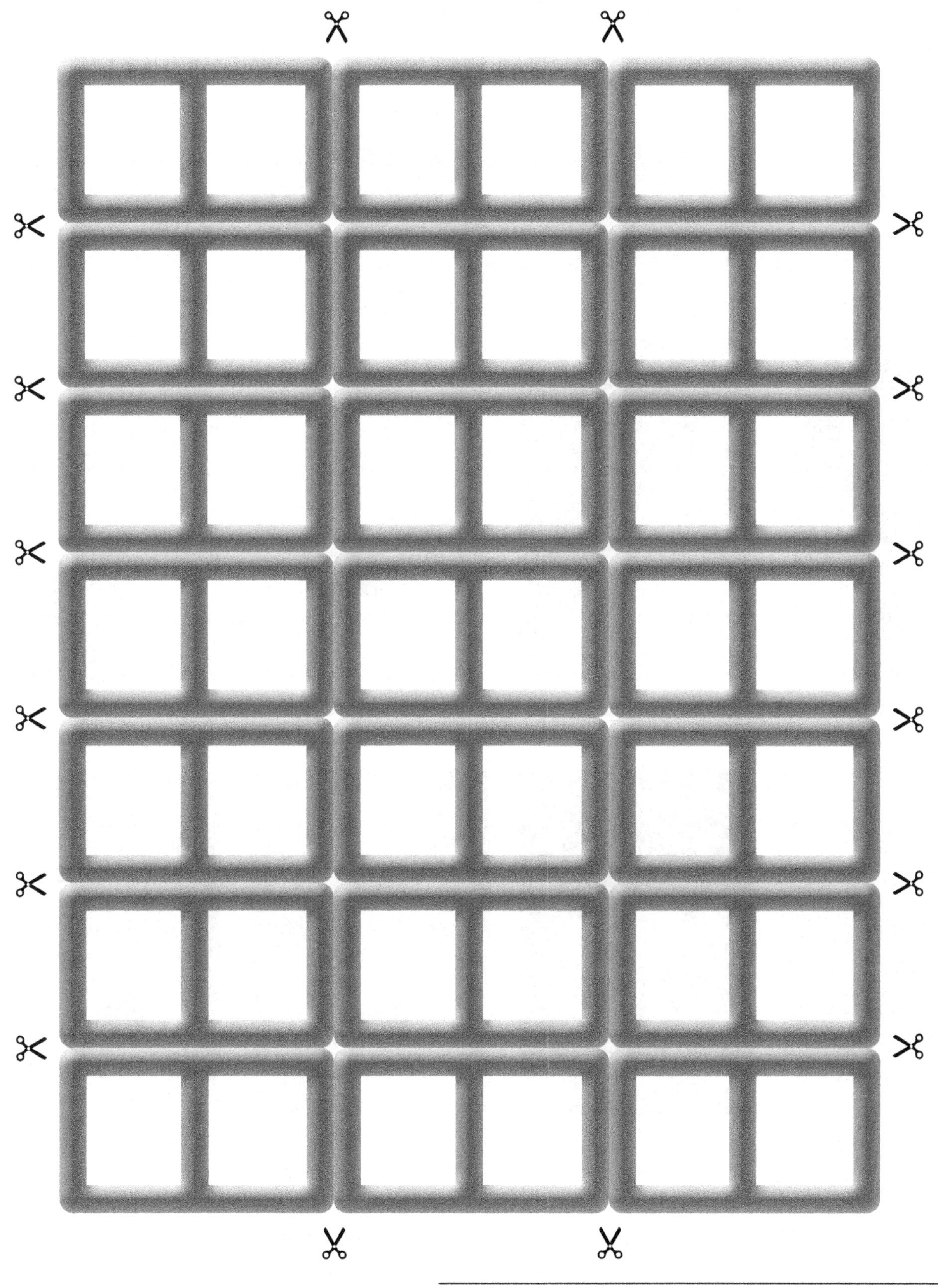

Tarquin

Also Available from Tarquin to enliven Junior Mathematical learning

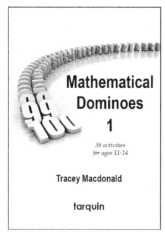

Mathematical Dominoes 1

First Tables Colouring

Second Tables Colouring

Arithmetic Arithmetic

Junior Mini Mathematical
Murder Mysteries

Junior Mathematical
Team Games

Junior Mathstraks Series: Books Available 7-8,
8-9, 9-10, 10-11 and Extension for 11+

Operation Order!

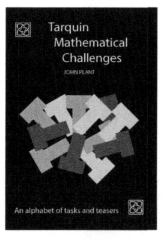

Tarquin Mathematical
Challenges

Ace Mathematical Games: Books Available for
Years 1,2,3,4,5,6

All texts available in paper and ebook form
www.tarquingroup.com and all good bookshops
Tarquin
Suite 74, 17 Holywell Hil,
St Albans, AL1 5JR, UK

Lightning Source UK Ltd.
Milton Keynes UK
UKOW07f1413180717
305539UK00003B/71/P